MAVERICK
A MEMOIR OF JACQUES KORNBROT
1938 - 2014

Battling through a traumatic childhood to lead an inspiring honourable life.

BY JACQUES KORNBROT AND DIANA JACOBS KORNBROT

Published by KornbrotOpen

Copyright © 2024 Diana Kornbrot

Cover design by: Catherine van Dyk

Expert proofreading by: Phil Clinker

Publication advice: Richard Chalmers

All rights reserved. No part of this publication may be reproduced, stored in a retrieval system, or transmitted in any form or by any means, electronic, mechanical, photocopy, recording or otherwise, without prior written permission of the copyright owner. Nor can it be circulated in any form of binding or cover other than that in which it is published and without similar condition including this condition being imposed on a subsequent purchaser.

ISBN: 978-1-7385095-0-8 Print on Demand
ISBN: 978-1-7385095-1-5 Ebook

KornbrotOpen is an imprint of

DolmanScott
www.dolmanscott.com

A memoir on how one individual battled through a traumatic transfer from a loving, competent foster family to a damaged, incompetent birth mother. A childhood with exposure to two countries, three religions, several education systems and conventional Jewish and Melbourne street societies. Alternate chapters are Jacques' autobiographical writings and my (his wife Diana's) description of the external historical context, and my own comfortable middle-class English experience for contrast. The story traces Jacques' life through an idyllic Second World War French village childhood, albeit occupied by the Nazis; a two-year primary school period, constrained by a depressed mother in a 6th floor Paris flat; a later childhood in Melbourne at state and private schools and with petty criminals. Early adult experience comprises Israeli kibbutzim, serving as a paratroop army officer, construction work and wide European travel. Later, he gained a medal in the 1967 Arab-Israel war. We met in the American Express in Athens in 1963 and married in 1973. We lived happily in a London suburb. Jacques became an avid and eclectic collector and influenced many friends of all ages in different societies and countries. This memoir aims to demonstrate how people with a traumatic start in life can go on to be a positive influence on many lives

DEDICATION

To Jacques Kornbrot

To: all the world's children facing hardship beyond their control

EPIGRAPH

All the world's a stage, and all the men and women merely players. They have their exits and their entrances; and one man in his time plays many parts.

Shakespeare

No coward soul is mine,
No trembler in the world's storm-troubled sphere:

Vain are the thousand creeds
That move men's hearts, unutterably vain.

With wide embracing love
The human spirit animates eternal years

Though Earth and moon were gone,
And suns and universes ceased to be,

There is not room for Death,
And what you gave may never be destroyed.

After Emily Brontë, although not what she believed!

CONTENTS

Chapter 1: Origins and early years, 1938-1945   **1**

Chapter 2: Jacques' writings: Villeherviers, Loire Valley, 1941-1945   **13**

Chapter 3: Primary school years, 1945-1948   **33**

Chapter 4: Jacques' writings: transition and Paris, 1945-1948   **41**

Chapter 5: Later childhood: Australia, England, 1946-1958   **53**

Chapter 6: Jacques' writings: Australia, 1948-1958   **63**

Chapter 7: Youth, 1958-1972: work, Israel, Europe, university, USA   **93**

Chapter 8: Jacques' writings: Israel, 1956-1972   **105**

Chapter 9: Jacques' reflections: parenting, childhood, social structure   **175**

Chapter 10: Jacques and Diana, London, 1972-2014   **211**

JACQUES' BIOGRAPHY 1938-2014

Childhood

Early infancy: October 1938 - January 1939
Jacques was born 22nd October 1938 in hospital, Paris XVIII.

His first three months were at 19 Rue Bachelet with mother and father. In January 1939, his mother was hospitalised with acute psychotic breakdown at the Asile de Ville-Evrard (21st January 1939 to 16th October 1945). His father was a 'garcon de chef' and was incarcerated at Pithiviers and deported to Auschwitz-Birkenau on 23rd September 1942, where he was murdered.

Wet nurse: January 1939 - Summer 1941
He has no memory of this time. He never met his father again.

Fostered: Thizeau Villeherviers, Loire et Cher, 1941-1945/6
Jacques was the much-loved youngest of four foster children living on a farm with animals. Primary school at Romarantin. Includes German occupation and contact with the Maquis.

Paris with hated mother and kind cousin: 6th floor, 1946-1948
Jacques was traumatised by separation from the foster family. He hated his mother and ran away frequently. He went to the local school and remembered getting into many fights.

Melbourne with hated mother, 1948-1956
Local primary school that ignored his lack of English. Frequently ran away. On advice of psychiatrists, sent to Ballarat grammar, a private boarding school that failed him. Summers sailing and swimming at luxury summer

home of relatives. Continually blamed for mother's miseries. Frequented Joe's Café, a haunt of petty criminals, but he did not participate.

Early Adulthood

A burgeoning independent adult: Israel, 1956-1961
Arrived in Israel with empty pockets and no Hebrew. He lived on Kibbutz Kissufim in the Negev and Eilot on the Red Sea. Met Willy Halpert, Australian friend, and founder of Aqua Sport.

From 1958 to 1961 he served in Israeli Defence Force; he was selected for officer school as a paratrooper. After a bad fall, he was assigned to the Nahal kibbutz Mashabei Sadeh.

After the army, 1961-1967
After the army, Jacques worked for a year as an agricultural worker on Kibbutz Negba.

Travels
First in Tel Aviv and then Europe, including France, Denmark, Russia, Germany, England.

Meeting
We met at the American Express in Athens. He picked up my fallen glasses and the rest is fabulous history. Jacques spent two months in London, and we became passionate lovers. We were not ready! He resumed his travels and returned to Israel and was working in Ashdod and Tel Aviv until 1967.

1967 war as reservist and aftermath, 1967-1972
Jacques was called up to the Gaza front in May 1967. His unit was supposed to 'mop up' after the action by the regular army. The initial push failed, and he found himself in the front line. He was wounded and treated. He

Jacques' Biography, 1938-2014

returned to battle and was again wounded and hospitalised for weeks with shrapnel in his back and wrists. He was decorated for bravery.

Aftermath of war
He recovered gradually. He spent time with Willy at Aqua Sport and on Kibbutz Negba. He spent time as an advisor in Kenya and the Congo. He ended up in Tel Aviv, leading a construction unit.

Reunited
We had continued corresponding and caught up after 1967. Contemplating his loss made me understand my great love. I visited Israel in Spring 1972. He proposed. I accepted with joy.

London: Marriage and later life, 1972-2014
We settled in East Finchley, a middle-class London suburb. Jacques had his own home and was immediately creative.

Employment
He worked initially as a consultant on motorway greenery, and then had other work, not using his talents. I progressed from Senior Lecturer to Head of Health & Human Sciences Research Institute, a Hertfordshire university. We were financially secure.

Creativity
He then devoted his energies to collecting items from car boot sales: African wood carvings, ugly mugs, tiles, ceramics, heads, etc. It is inspiring to live with the eclectic results.

Travel
Our first trip was America. We toured all France, failing to find Jacques' foster family, who he then traced via his Paris school, and was reunited with his foster sister. He visited Israel every year. Travel for work and pleasure also included Denmark, Italy, Turkey, Spain, Portugal, Australia, Thailand.

Social
Friends, and their children, came from Israel, Denmark, Australia, America, France. Jacques embraced my family: mother, grandmother, brothers and their children. He made strong new friendships in several different societies: neighbours, shops, gym, work, my friends.

Rachel Msetfi, initially my Ph.D. student, and Muffi, a Moroccan French speaker, became particular friends.

Death: 6th November 2014
Jacques had three bouts of pneumonia from June 2014, but we did not know it was serious. Then he was diagnosed with cancer of the immune system. He was admitted with a fourth infection that took rapid hold. The Royal Free did their best for him in intensive care, but he never regained consciousness. I hope somewhere he heard me say how much I loved him.

- Jacques led an honourable, creative, positive life

PERSONAE

People who had an impact on Jacques' life.
Families are indicated by top and bottom lines.
Locations are where Jacques mostly knew them but may include origins.
Roughly in the order Jacques came to know them.

Diana's family[1]

Edmonde Jacobs	Mother	London
Sarah London	Grandmother	London
Tim Jacobs[11]	Brother: engineer, art entrepreneur	Glasgow
Lynne Jacobs	Sister-in-law: GP	Glasgow
Richard Jacobs	Nephew: Rabbi	Jerusalem
Nicola Mellman	Niece: maths, management	Chicago
Philip Jacobs	Nephew: consultant anaesthetist	Glasgow
Myke Jacobs[12]	Brother: lawyer, charity, civic	London
Ruth Jacobs[13]	Sister-in-law: magistrate, charity	London
Ben Jacobs	Nephew: lawyer	Auckland
Alex Jacobs	Nephew: Chinese medicine	London
Reuben Finkelstein[14]	Grandma Sarah's cousin	California
Leland Finkelstein[15]	Son California	
Linda, Andrea, Nancy	Leland's children	USA
Raymond Itelsohn[16]	Son Grandma sister Marguerite	Paris
Georgette Austern	Daughter Grandma sister Dora	Paris
Roger, Regina Pinto[17]	Distant cousins	Paris
Gilbert, Yves Pinto	Sons, Roger, Regina	Paris
Liliane, Dedi Pinto	Daughters-in-law, Regina, Roger	Paris, Nice
Stefan Pinto	Son, Yves, Dedi	Switzerland
Elise Beedle[18]	Paternal aunt, 1 child	UK
Val Simon[19]	Paternal aunt, 8,children	UK
Suzanne Hayes[110]	Paternal aunt, 1 child	UK, NZ
Yair Regev[111]	Son grandpa's sister Tova	Israel
Rachel Konigsberg[112]	Daughter murdered sister Grandpa	Poland

xiii

Maverick: A memoir of Jacques Kornbrot, 1938 - 2014

Jacques' birth family[2]

Joseph Kornbrot[21]	Father: murdered at Auschwitz	Warsaw, Paris
Marie Rockman[22]	Mother: remarried after 1956	Warsaw, Melbourne
Rose Woolf[23]	Aunt	Poland, Tel Aviv
Ray Rockman[24]	Second cousin, lawyer	Melbourne
Norman Rockman[25]	Far cousin. Arranged Ballarat	Melbourne
Susie Rockman[26]	Wife of Norman	Melbourne
Irvin Rockman[27]	Son, Norman, Susie: Lord Mayor	Melbourne

Jacques' possible paternal family[3]

Kornbrots	Holocaust survivors	Poland, USA
Anna Kornbrot[31]	Daughter: maxillary surgeon	USA
Barry Klayman	Son-in-law: lawyer	USA
Alison Klayman[32]	Daughter, Anna, Barry: film, podcast	USA

Jacques' foster family[4]

Thizeau	Foster parents	Villeherviers
Marcelle Thizeau	Foster daughter	Loire
Denise Pouradier[41]	Adopted daughter: post office, chef	Romarantin
Henri Pouradier	Forester	Romarantin
Francine Ferlet[42]	Daughter, Denise, Henri: couture	Paris
Christian	Son, Denise, Henri: nurse, horses	Lannemezan
Martine	Daughter, Denise, Henri	Orleans

Personae

Overseas[5]

Willy Halpert[51]	Aqua Sport, diver, coach	Australia, Israel
Mordi Zorea[52]	Army, Locksmith, football referee	Holon
Freda Zorea	Army	Holon
Amitai Shecter	Army, Computers,	Tel Aviv
Dany Hai	Army, Agriculture	Beersheba
Amos Gur	Army, Psychologist	Jerusalem
Batya Gur	Divorced Amos: writer	Jerusalem
Ilana Tsaba-Winer[53]	Army Jacques almost married,	Israel
Kuba Vilan[54]	Kibbutz head, Member Knesset	Negba
Gershon Vilan[55]	Agriculture	Negba
Abu Vilan[56]	Peace Now Member Knesset	Negba
Eitan Ariele[57]	Agriculture, plastics factory	Negba
Drori Lamdan[58]	Agriculture, plastics factory	Negba
Ariele Lamdan	Academic, women's issues	Negba
Roberta Stock[59]	Computer entrepreneur, academic	Tel Aviv
Ilona Zevulun[510]	Teacher	Herzliya
Avishai Zevulun	Judge	Herzliya
Dario	Optician	Tel A
Henning Mortensen[511]	Novelist	Aarhus, Dane
Gadoulets[512]	Vintners, African Eurocrat	Lons, France
Batya Amit	Maths teacher, academic	Israel

UK friends[6]

Laurie Brown[61]	BWD, construction, consulting	Australia, London
Tim Mclagan[62]	Ski shop	Finchley
Teresa Maclagan	Director, smart card industry	Finchley
Ian Wood[63]	Builder	Dover
Theresa Wood	Special needs	Dover
Ellen Orans Morgan[64]	Autism, City University	London, NYC
Wally Morgan	Jeweller, social worker	London
Local Barber	Long Lane	Finchley
Local	Café, Muswell Hill	Finchley
Alan	Record shop	Finchley

Maverick: A memoir of Jacques Kornbrot, 1938 - 2014

Diana: KAS[7](King Alfred School)

Dalia Ziegler Charles[71]	Designer, artist	Hampstead
Faustin Charles[72]	Caribbean poet, novelist: child write	Hampstead
Juliet Mitchell[73]	Author, psychoanalyst	Cambridge
Riva Joffe[74]	Gender psychotherapy, left activist	London
Howard Cheek	Businessman	New Forest
Peter Lipton	Biologist, academic	Madison
Sidney Thompson	Surveyor	Amersham

Diana Professional Friends[8] UH* is Hertfordshire University

Gene Galanter[81]	Academic, entrepreneur, supervisor	Columbia Uni
John Molino	Fellow student, NSF Washington	Columbia Uni
Jock Owens[82]	Fellow student, amateur pilot	Columbia Uni
Scott Parker[83]	Fellow student, brief relationship	G W Uni
Noel Lawler	Technical	UH*
Amanda Sacker[84]	Ph.D. Head Research Unit,	UH* Essex Uni
Richard Wiseman[85]	Popular open science, magician	UH* Edinburg
Lia Kvavilashvili[86]	Episodic memory	UH* Georgia
George Georgiou [87]	Ph.D. Cyber computing	UH*
Rachel Msetfi[88]	Ph.D. Contingency. VP Research	Maynooth Uni
Muffi Msetfi[89]	Chef	Ireland
Mike Page[812]	Memory, climate, cube eco house	UH* Barnet
John Long[810]	Head Ergonomic Unit UCL	Muswell Hill
Doris Long	Wife John	Muswell Hill
Mark Elliot	Psychophysics colleague	Galway Uni
Elena Kulinskaya[811]	Russian statistician	E. Anglia Uni
George Myasoedov	Husband of Elena, collector	Norwich

Diana: Bristol friends[9]

Dilys Jenkins	BSc Physics, teacher,	Australia
Jean White	BSc Physics Diverse, spiritual,	York
Valerie Cleverton[91]	BA German Academic literature	Bari Italy
Carole Buick[92]	BA History Editor, EFL>immigrants	Clapham
Richard Fries[93]	Chess with Jacques, civil servant	Clapham
Beryl Thomas	BA English	Wales

Neighbours[1]

Mrs Allen[101]	80+ widow, nurse 1st neighbour	Elmhurst
Loulla Watson[102]	Fitness, gardener	Talbot
Pat Petrie[103]	Social pedagogue, academic UCL	Elmhurst
Glen Petrie	Historian, writer	Elmhurst
Helen Pettifor[104]	Educationalist	Elmhurst
Richard Pettifor	Biologist	Elmhurst
Sue Loughnane[105]	Accountant	Elmhurst
Simon Kavanagh	Copywriter	Elmhurst
David Sagal[106]	Computer, charity	Talbot
Jane Sagal	Teacher	Talbot
Mary O'Toole	Social worker	Elmhurst
Charles O'Toole	Social worker	Elmhurst
Joe Crouch	Cellist	Elmhurst
Wiebke Crouch	Musician, academic	Elmhurst
Jenny Cohen	Actor	Talbot
Naomi Zeitlin	Photographer	Trinity
Joanna Michlic	East Europe, Holocaust historian	Elmhurst
Catherine Hopper	Singer	Elmhurst
Sam Evans	Musician	Elmhurst

ACKNOWLEDGEMENTS

Writing about the real world is tough, much tougher than academic Mss. I owe an enormous debt of gratitude to the many people who supported me through this endeavour, commented on drafts, gave strategic advice, and encouraged me as I laboured on over years and months. First to Carole Buick Fries, a friend from Bristol University who had been a professional editor and was making insightful comments until a week before she died of pancreatic cancer. Then to my indefatigable brother Myke and sister-in-law Ruth, who rephrased awkward sentences, corrected WORD's grammar checker and, most importantly, gave strategic help and focus to all the context chapters and on our life together in London. Then to Willy Halpert, who had known Jacques in his teens in Melbourne and through his time in Eilat and afterwards in London. He had many humorous anecdotes, too many to include all in the book. Then to friends who were themselves published authors. To Faustin Charles, who has written in many genres and introduced me to professional publishers Dolman Scott. To Richard Wiseman, who writes on popular as well as academic science and guided me in attempting to focus on potential readers. To John Long, who provided photos form his blog and could comment on how Jacques appeared to his contemporaries. To Pat Petrie, our much-loved next-door neighbour who had written on child pedagogy and has known Jacques for 40 years from our first days in Elmhurst . To Rachel Msetfi, who had key insights on childhood hardship and our life together. Pictures To Alison Klayman, Jacques' newly discovered possible cousin who provided expert photos. To all our friends who shared photos that have been incorporated in the final Ms. Finally, to Phil Clinker, who did a brilliant job of proofreading, to Richard Chalmers of Dolman Scott, who expertly and patiently guided me through publishing my first book, and to Catherine van Dyk designer.

FOREWORD: RICHARD WISEMAN

I have known Diana for many years, and so it is a delight to be asked to write this short foreword. This book is a loving and thorough account of a fascinating life. It describes Jacques' remarkable journey across the globe and the dramatic influence that he had on those he encountered. But more than that, it also provides a revealing and insightful glimpse into his inner world, including the many ways in which he coped with difficulties, flourished in the face of adversity and developed his unique and quirky way of approaching life. Part memoir and part social history, Diana is to be congratulated on doing a remarkable job of bringing the material together and providing a valuable sense of perspective and context. Together, this is an informative read that provides us with a portal into the past and shows how we are all shaped by and in our turn influence our surroundings.

PREFACE

This book is a work of love and homage. Jacques, when he was settled in his thirties and beyond, wrote to express his own recollections of what had been important in his life, and what might be of importance to others. At the time he did not seem to want to discuss his writing, although we did discuss many of the episodes that he recounts, some humorous, some bitter. So, the writings amplified my understanding rather than producing new knowledge. Now, I so wish I had pressed him to talk more, and even to publish in his own lifetime. His writing is a varied mixture of personal recollections and reflections about how the world might be changed for the better, particularly if the adult world listened to children. In this book I try to transmit the messages he wanted the world to hear, as well as to amuse and entertain.

To me, the book is a striking memoir of 20th and 21st century life in various parts of the West (including Australia, as is common practice). There is a contrast between my comfortable middle-class life and Jacques' sometimes traumatic experiences. His is a view from adulthood about childhood experience. There is no reason to doubt his accounts of events, e.g. accidentally lying down on a bee's nest, or of daily living. After 30 years apart, his foster sister confirmed everything, including things that may have seemed unlikely: 'it was a quiet house; no one ever shouted' a golden halo? No. Completely accurate according to Denise; 'the foster parents were old', you were a kid, all adults looked old. No, they *were* old – see chapter 1 picture, about a year after Jacques left.

This book may appeal to many different interests. One audience is people who knew Jacques, another is people who like a good story. More than that, there is meat for people who are interested in childhood experience and/or idealists trying to build a new country and a more just society. Finally, there is core material for health and social professionals. Jacques would have liked his experiences to inform how psychiatrists deal with any child and how social workers deal with children of inadequate or missing parents, and, of course, the training and law that underpins their actions. Jacques provides numerous examples of 'blame the victim'.

Structure

The structure is unusual. It comprises alternate chapters (even numbers) of Jacques' own writings with surrounding chapters (odd numbers) providing context. It is a memoir not a history, so the context chapters (odd numbers) include world events that influenced our lives google, and personae information via numbered notes.

In summary, the Second World War came and went, socialist ideas were tried with varied success. Jacques experienced a happy early childhood with a foster family, a disastrous later childhood with an inadequate mother followed by life In Israel on several kibbutzim, and work and travel. Reading his account provides insights into childcare and fostering and helps explain why the idealist kibbutz movement failed.

Chapter 2 describes a rural French childhood that was 'idyllic' in spite of an occupying Nazi army. It also describes the confusions that occur when the adults and children viewed that occupation so very differently. How children cope with these confusions is part of growing up that should be of interest to child psychologists. Chapter 4 describes the trauma of being ripped from a loving and competent foster family and placed with a severely damaged birth mother. Jacques still somehow managed to make relationships: with the old lady in the window across the courtyard, with the gendarmes who picked him up and had a singsong. He fought in school to defend himself, but did not seem to have any idea why he was being attacked or why others liked fighting. There are lessons here for health and social professionals. There are yet more lessons in chapter 6, where he recounts his experiences of state and private schools, well-intentioned relatives, and what seemed to him (and to me) useless psychiatrists. Then he becomes an adult, thrown into the burgeoning state of Israel, chapter 8. He sees kibbutz life, warts and all. He notes the frustrations of the competent and the power of group pressure. The army discovered he had leadership talents and made him a paratroop officer. Israel was the first place since the Loire Valley that he experienced people valuing him. Still, he had curiosity about all the world and set off to travel Europe. His writings include *nothing* about the army or the European travel, or later about his consultancy in Africa. He had many anecdotes but did not feel the need to write them down. Maybe they were non-problematic? The final part of chapter 8 describes his role in the 1967 Arab-Israel war, a war of survival for Israel in which he took honourable part. He was horrified by the aftermath, particularly the West Bank Settlements, often by right-wing religious American zealots. It was not what he and his army and kibbutz friends had fought for. He was equally horrified by Netanyahu, and that a small number of his friends had even taken that direction. Chapter 9 is a rather rambling collection of reflections from all parts of his life. Chapter 10 describes our life together and how Jacques' stories and example became important to so many people, young and old.

Communication

As I read and re-read Jacques' words. I am struck by his desperate need to communicate and the fact that I never realized its strength. He did not seem to want to talk about his writing, so I did not press him. It is an eternal regret. We should have written this book together, it would have been so much better, but I am where I am alone so this is the best I can do.

- I was so lucky to have Jacques as a lover, friend, and inspiration.

Reading notes

In Jacques' chapters my comments are inset in italics. The epub version has blue links to external places and places and events, and to people who influenced Jacques' life described under *Personae*. Readers of the paper version may obtain external informati

CHAPTER 1.
ORIGINS AND EARLY YEARS 1938 -1945

Jacques' origins

Poland and France, origins
The 20th century had arrived in Warsaw. In the years before the First World War, Joseph Kornbrot was born in 1902 and Marie Rochman in 1909. World War One was raging throughout their childhood.

Jacques' maternal family
Marie Rochman was one of several children of Osher ben Zvi: oldest sister Rose Woolf, who emigrated to Melbourne in August 1939 (just in time), brothers Yaacov (Adele, Ian, Ray's grandfather) and another brother Moshe, who died in Paris during the Second World War and was father of Jacques' cousin Jacques, who he lived with during his Paris years. Marie's brothers were successful in the Australian garment business. Some cousins were very successful in the property sector (Norman and son Irvin, Lord Mayor of Melbourne 1977-79). Aunt Rose said Joseph was a 'Don Juan' with many lady friends. I have not been able to find anything else about him. Still looking.

Jacques' parents' early years
As the 20s and 30s progressed, then, as now, many inhabitants left Warsaw for some golden dream. Joseph got to Paris via Belgium and worked as a cook or waiter. Marie and her older sister Rose, and at least one other brother, chose Paris. I do not know what Marie did, but she met Joseph and started an affair. She became pregnant around February or March 1938. In April, Joseph and Marie were married in a Paris Synagogue.

Maverick: A memoir of Jacques Kornbrot, 1938 - 2014

Jacques' parents 1938. Joseph, Marie

They then lived together in Rue Bachelet, with Marie's sister Rose and her husband and brother, with son Jacques. Were Joseph and Marie living together before marriage? I do not know. Rue Bachelet is the residence of Dora Bruder's parents described in the docunovel by Nobel Laureate Patrick Modiano. Marie was not happy to be expecting.

Jacques' arrival and infancy

Jacques arrived on 22nd October 1938 in a hospital, Paris XVIII, after a difficult birth. Marie would not open her eyes. She returned home in a state of major depression. Her family must have tried to help and look after Jacques. Things got progressively worse, and in January 1939 Marie had a full-blown schizophrenic breakdown, screaming and hallucinating in the street. She was committed to a mental hospital (under the name of Rochman, perhaps because there was no civil wedding) on 20th January 1939 in Paris, then Hopital Ste Anne, Ville-Evrard 21, later that month. Her symptoms were psychotic: hallucinations and demented behaviour. She remained in ignorance of the Second World War. The hospital recorded all visits and letters to and from Marie, also known as Cuiji. She made repeated appeals for release and to see her son. She was released on 16th October 1945, more than a year after the liberation of Paris. Her husband made a visit 'affecteuse (affectionate)' on 27th April 1939. On 2nd September 1939 World War 2 broke out.

CHAPTER 1: ORIGINS AND EARLY YEARS, 1938-1945

Joseph, Jacques' father, was interned at Pithiviers detention camp on 14th May 1941 and deported to Auschwitz on 25th June 1942, where he was murdered. There is no evidence of contact between Joseph and Marie after April 1939. Lettre cachetée (sealed) à Monsieur KORNBROT Camp 2- Baraque 12. Pithiviers ([probably a letter from Marie to Joseph that was not deliverable).

World War 2 starts

Maverick: A memoir of Jacques Kornbrot, 1938 - 2014

I learned about the asylum eight months after Jacques died, when I was contacted by Corinne Benestroff, a psychoanalytic therapist who was researching the experiences of migrants in mental hospitals during the Second World War and the reactions of their relatives. Corinne arranged for me to access (but not copy) the asylum records, and we became friends. Jacques had no idea about the asylum. He knew only that his mother was too mentally ill to take care of him. She *chose* not to tell him. Other members of the family respected her decision. As always, the mother's wishes came before Jacques' welfare. He noted that for seven years she had made no attempt to contact him and showed no obvious concern for him.

Jacques' early life

Jacques was sent to a nourice (wet nurse) in the Loire valley, Mme Girard. He remembered *nothing* of that time. This supports him being fostered at rising three (harvest time, 1941) rather than later. Presumably, father Joseph and Marie's sister(s) and brother were unable to take care of him. Or perhaps social services deemed them 'unfit'? Who knows? Mme Girard, the nourice, visited the asylum in February 1943, but there was no mention of an infant. Jacques had almost certainly already been given to the Thizeau foster family by then. It is really weird that there is nothing in the asylum records. Jacques' birth and early fostering were *not* due to the war.

The authorities seem to have lost track of Jacques' whereabouts. "9 mai 1944: Lettre au médecin. La nourrice explique qu'elle a déposé Jacques KORNBROT au centre de la Selle sur Cher. En post-scriptum: « J'espère que Madame Rochman a reçu le petit colis que je lui avis retourné." She does not say WHEN she gave Jacques to services at Selle sur Cher. However, it was before the liberation of Paris in August 1944. Jacques had no conscious memory of his time with the wet nurse. There is a record of 28th December 1943: "Lettre à Joseph ROCHMAN [Marie's brother]. Mention « retour à l'envoyeur-décédé ». Salle admission. Lit 36. Hôpital

CHAPTER 1: ORIGINS AND EARLY YEARS, 1938-1945

Broussais 96, rue Dido." This conflicts with the story told to Jacques about his uncle being taken by the Germans, while his cousin hid in the toilet.

Marie lodged with Joseph's son Jacques when she was released. The asylum knew about his father's death, but when is unclear. "Comme suite à votre note citée en référence, j'ai l'honneur de vous faire connaître que le juif Kornbrot Joseph, né le 17 avril 1902 à Varsovie, de nationalité polonaise, demeurant 19, rue Bachelet à Paris 16ème a quitté le 23 septembre 1942, pour une destination inconnue, le camp de Pithiviers où il était interné." Destination 'inconnue'! The French authorities did not want to know, but at least they saved Marie, and many like her.

Meanwhile, in the Loire Valley.

Villeherviers: a happy early childhood

For three or four years, Jacques was fostered in the tiny hamlet of Villeherviers now population 484, near Romorantin-Lanthenay in the Loire-et-Cher. His mother reclaimed him in late 1945 or early 1946. Jacques remembers snow on the ground at her first visit, but was not clear how long it was before he was sent to Paris. All contact with the foster family was completely cut off. This was the custom in those days. In any event, they were illiterate, so communication would have been difficult.

We did not find Villeherviers and reconnect with Jacques' foster sister Denise until 1973. They fell into each other's arms. Some of Jacques' writings and longing to return predate the reunion. What is remarkable is how well their memories coincided, even after 30 years with no opportunity for joint embellishment.

Earliest memories, awakening

Jacques' earliest memories are of being in hospital eating a very big fish. He thinks he was two or three years old. If so, it would have been summer

5

1941. He had no conscious memory of anything before that. For him it was an 'awakening'. I am not sure how common that is. I have early memories embedded in daily routine, but no 'instance of awakening'. Most early memories are like that, fleeting glimpses of places, people, or events. Nothing as epochal as: 'As I can recall the awakening to my environment, I had the knowledge that I wasn't the only one there. Yes, that was my first encounter with life.' I have found one other similar experience in the compelling biography of Jan Morris, *Conundrum*. This period is the foundation of Jacques' identity, as a loved member of a family, but with his own personal views. At this stage, there is no hint of a feeling of being other.

Daily life and recurrent events
Jacques was welcomed into the Thizeau family farm in the woods seven kilometres from Romarantin. He was the 'flower' of the family with middle-aged foster parents, sister Denise (+8 years), red-haired brother (+8 years) and elder sister Marcel with learning difficulties. A peaceful, happy, and secure life is central to his memories, which include: the farmhouse, the family, daily living, play, grape harvests, festivals, starting school.

Arrival of Germans and the consequences
Jacques and Denise encountered adult complexities. What made people 'goodies' or 'baddies'? Friendly, clean (if incomprehensible) German soldiers arrived in trucks, not welcomed by parents. The Maquis, dishevelled and unshaven Resistance fighters, were welcomed and fed. It is illuminating to have a child's view of such complexities, not often available.

Looking back on early experiences
These include a yearning for his early happy childhood. He talks about religion and its lack of effect on human happiness and welfare. He reflects

CHAPTER 1: ORIGINS AND EARLY YEARS, 1938-1945

on the different stages in a human life. He considers the effects of war in general and the Second World War in particular. He wants to know more about other children with lives disrupted by war.

Diana's origins

England leading up to the Second World War

Harry Jacobs and Edmonde London had a posh traditional wedding in July 1938 at Golders Green Synagogue. They went on honeymoon to Venice at the time of the Biennale and bought a stunning nude picture by de Chirico, later sold by Edmonde, as widow, to meet expenses.

Diana's parents wedding 1938. Harry, Edmonde, groups

In August 1939, they visited Denmark, where I was conceived, returning on the last boat out before the war began. The extended family (at least 11) took a house in Brighton. Harry enlisted. Edmonde and Harry moved away from Brighton's social hubbub to the intimacy and quiet of the village of Clandon, where I was born on 25th May 1940. Harry went back to his unit (anti-aircraft, ack-ack) and officer training, in Wales and elsewhere.

England in the Second World War

Edmonde's parents, Sarah and Solomon London, had moved into a big house in North Oxford (21 St Margaret's Road), accompanied by Edmonde and me. Harry, still based in the UK, visited occasionally on leave and Timothy arrived at the Radcliffe Hospital on 30th October 1942, when I was two and a half. I have vague memories of mother going into hospital and then of Tim being there in the cot in the bedroom at the top of the house. No memories of mother changing shape, or of being informed of pending arrival, or of actual arrival at the house. Early on, Edmonde worked for the ophthalmologist teaching department at hospital. She was also an air-aid warden.

My early life: Oxford exile in the war

I was aware of war, and of the importance of the BBC news. I knew about bombs, but thought they dropped bits and pieces (shrapnel) rather than exploding. Like Jacques, I remember salient events and isolated incidents. I was due to be bridesmaid for my mother's first cousin Rachel (4th July 1944). Endless fitting for dress, standing on a chair while the dressmaker took pins from her mouth to mark the hem. Very hard to stand still (that has not changed).

Who am I?

I already started to feel 'other'. These weird adults believed in an afternoon nap! Up to bedroom, strip to underclothes, into bed. As soon as they left, I could return to a favourite fantasy: being an aeroplane rushing round the room with arms outstretched. As soon as the safety gate at the top of the stairs clicked, I leapt back to bed, shut my eyes and reverted to 'good girl'. I needed to be very sure they closed the gate, so that any adult approach could be heard. (They never figured it out but were 'puzzled', I learnt later.)

I was always curious about how things worked. I received an antique doll for my fifth birthday. Its eyes opened and shut. If one pushed the left eye in, the right eye popped out, and vice versa. What happens if one pushes both eyes in? Consternation from adults about state of antique doll. To this day I can feel my mouth opening to explain, then I looked at their faces and shut my mouth. 'Forget it,' I thought, 'they will *never* understand.' I felt 'other' then and continued to do so throughout my life.

A more fun (and sensible) fifth birthday present was a kitten I named Fluffy. She subsequently had a kitten of her own. I thought it would enjoy the garden, but Fluffy thought otherwise and kept on taking it back to her blanket. I can still hear Fluffy moaning pitifully. Several trips back and forth before my mother firmly announced that Fluffy knew best about *her* baby. Another mismatch of child and adult views. My mother failed to mention that Fluffy was not a totally ideal mother. She had already consumed several offspring in the airing cupboard before they rescued the final lucky one. The cats did not migrate to London with us, and I never had any more pets other than goldfish (boring and short-lived acquisitions from Easter/Whitsun fairs).

Salient memories
My other salient memories include following Grandpa around on the eve of Pesah as he ritually, with candle, looked for homatz (bread) that he had just placed in hidden spots. Weird but fun. I had been told about God, who made us all. I went to sleep musing on infinite regress of a God who made God, and a God who made that God. Actual God was pretty insignificant by the time I got to sleep. I also told myself night-time stories, where a leader, perhaps an ancestor, had an enormous cloak with pockets that

served as a residence for all the characters and events. I rolled to sleep between bedclothes and side of bed as the imaginary cloak. Physical realism did not enter this fantasy.

Religion
I have no memory of synagogue or prayers of any kind. Later, I learnt that Grandpa was host to many Jewish intellectuals: Max Gombrich, Isaiah Berlin, Ernst Chain. I so regret never having met any of them, but it was past my bedtime. Later, my grandparents kept up with the Chains. Jacques told Ernst that the Mexicans had discovered penicillin with a completely straight face; neither Ernst nor I knew if he was aware – of course he was!

Visits
Daddy came intermittently and took me for a ride in a *car* – quite an event! Grandpa Hymie (paternal) took me for boat rides on the Isis. Grandma Rai (paternal) visited with great-grandma and companion Na. My memory is confused between great-grandma (who died soon after) and Na (who was part of later childhood).

Nursery school
I loved it. I learnt to read. Apparently, I was thrilled by the discovery of the letter 'e' and scrawled it all over home walls – not that I remember. I do recall enthusiastic trike riding following two bigger boys. Don't remember school interior, or other kids. Apparently, Dorothy Hodgkin's children were there. Oxford was an intellectual powerhouse. But how many Oxford townsfolk participated?

Childhood experience

The Second World War raged throughout our childhood. While our parents faced the anxieties and miseries of war, we both had a happy time of it. We had families who were unthinkingly loving as a matter of course: hours of stimulating play (solo and with other kids), exciting communal events (harvest, Christmas, Passover). My life continued that way, while Jacques' hit the buffers amid the horrors of a disastrous relocation.

About Chapter 2, Villeherviers

Jacques' writings are organised into several themes, including specific episodes, daily life, and reflections. Some writing predates finding his foster sister Denise and the farmhouse on the outskirts of Villeherviers.

- First awareness: Hospital, nurses, big fish. Foster parents arrive.
- Daily life: Farmhouse. Household. Food. Play. Acting grown-up.
- Rhythm of life: Harvests, Christmas. Easter. Sunday.
- Confusions of adult world, German occupiers and the Maquis.
- Reflections looking back on Villeherviers.

CHAPTER 2.
JACQUES' WRITINGS, VILLEHERVIERS

Awakening: Life begins…

As I can recall the awakening to my environment, I had the knowledge that I wasn't the only one there. Yes, that was my first encounter with life. The atmosphere was filled with noises of people talking to me. It sounded like bees burbling in this gigantic room. Women in white walking about and laughing as they went by, the bright shining of the sun through the left side of the window. I looked up. I was in this big ward with more beds than I could count. Men of all ages, I was the smallest one there. Nothing made sense. At those times the ward was run by nuns, pretty old ones.

At 11am – or was it midday? – a gargantuan fish was brought for me on a plate on a tray, the biggest fish you could imagine. It was the first meal I can remember. I was only two and a half or three years old. I stared down and looked and looked. Whether I ate, I don't remember, but I felt good all over with all those nuns rushing by.

Meeting foster parents and arrival at the farm
Then, in the late afternoon, my foster parents turned up. A group of people crowded around the bed – and they smiled and talked to me, trying very hard to make themselves understood. The middle-aged couple came to my bed and stood there, and I was told they were my parents.

Maverick: A memoir of Jacques Kornbrot, 1938 - 2014

Thizeau foster parents 1946

They looked upon me with joy and kept on smiling. So, at the time I thought they were my real parents, plus a brother and two sisters. We were the last four that they fostered. My kindness comes from them and nobody else. They dressed me.

Was he in pyjamas before? Where did the clothes come from?

No nourice goodbye? No conscious memories, good or bad.

I was taken out and my father put me on his bike, walking by the side. It was great, but not comfortable being high up there and trying to stay on. They all walked as the sun was at the back of us. The landscape was beautiful, with green trees in front. We were heading towards the trees and at the edge of them, straight on the path of two roads, was a farmhouse. One road leading for the forest – the other I don't know. It was very beautiful. As they opened the gate, there were animals rushing about and a big goat tied up and this very big black dog.

No Germans.

CHAPTER 2: JACQUES' WRITINGS: VILLEHERVIERS, LOIRE VALLEY, 1941-1945

We had finally arrived at the house on the edge of the woods. Looking around was dog! I did not know that this would be my home for a few years to come – would I have thought about it at the time?

Life on the Loire Valley farm

Daily life
Although the Second World War was in action, it was peaceful for a time. It was my road to my short childhood, with fine people that during their lifetime had fostered 45 kids.

The farmhouse: location and routine
Oh yes, I still have not described the Farm. On the edge of the forest, village maybe three or four miles from town, was our four-room house. To the right was a hut where the wood would be stored, and along the side of the house was where the goat, chicken, and the animals lived. Between the house and the hut was a small pond and the forest, and behind the house was the field, and you could see far into the distance except for a large tree in the centre of the field and the remains of a bomber; it was situated on the side of the forest – as you come from the fields.

Villeherviers farm

Yes, the seven kilometres square we lived in had everything: Germans, the Maquis, farmers, a crashed bomber. We had what you could call the good life: no running water, electricity – all those modern things. Though it was in an area where all the French kings lived. I never saw a chateau till years later. They are very well hidden. any toys at all. I didn't miss toys until later when I was joining the system.

> But Father Christmas brought him SOMETHING. His focus was on the existence, or not, of Father Christmas, not on the presents.

Household members and activities
Their name was *Tissot*; I don't know whether that was the way it was written. I became a kid, the smallest of them all, my two big sisters, one was a very strange one, the other one and my brother's red hair, and I was number four. A child, the youngest and the most wanted.

Foster Family 1941/2. Denise, Marcel, Jacques, brother

I don't think we have ever gone away hungry from the table. Was it because it was peaceful? One would never get blood pressure there. My mother was the nicest person one could have. Every morning, she would dress me and make me do the holy cross. Then we had breakfast. I would go afterwards to play in the woods with my two supposed sisters and brother. One sister was handicapped, and she would help in the house, then take the goats to the nearby field to graze.

Name was Thizeau, we discovered later.

Food
We all did something to get all sorts of food. There were all kind of animals around. The house was very well situated nearby a pond that we fished for frogs. I don't remember eating them, or the small birds and rabbits that were caught. But the bangers we had with mashed potatoes or the horrible wine soup with old bread, that I remember very well indeed. Never got used to it. Yet food was not a major thing for me.

Catching birds
It was my first education on how to catch food without being frozen. Papa would sit in the kitchen holding the rope, then would pull the door on those birds that would come for shelter and grain that he had laid there. Yank! The door would come down and he would rush out and jump on the door to make sure they were all dead. I would rush after him and jump on the door. There was always something interesting going on.

Fishing
Oh, I learned about life there. In spring the ice would melt, and the greenery would come. Everybody would have a pole and string attached and a hook on it – and go towards the pond that was next to the house and fish frogs out of it for dinner. Exactly how or what one must use to catch a frog was beyond me, but I knew that once you got one you would strip him of his skin, then put the skin on the hook, repeating it until you had a dish full, and then the lady of the house would make a

terrific meal. How we survived during those times is still a mystery but we came through.

German bomber
On one winter night we were awakened by a big bang. Next day, a big bomber was about 200 yards away, all burned up. My father took off to see what mess it had made of the potato field we had planted a week ago. He came back saying that it surely made a really big hole and that he wouldn't have to dig out all the potatoes and plant them in another place. Then he looked at me, saying that I should never go there because it was dangerous. I didn't know what was dangerous. I remember Mama also telling us that we should not go to the crashed bomber, although we did. After a couple of months my big brother and I went and played around it anyway. It was gigantic from one end to the other.

Acting grown-up – making the fire
Every morning was nearly the same. My Papa went straight to the fireplace and cleaned away the ashes so he could get to some of the charcoal, still alight. Then he would put some paper over it and with a long iron pole that had a hole going right through, blew right in it – that was the way I understood the fire started – at the same time my mother would put wood in the cooker and take fire from the fireplace. Well, one morning I awoke before everyone and dressed myself. While dressing I started to do the same thing that my Papa did. I cleaned away the ashes and got a piece of paper – then put the paper into the heavy oven, placing it right underneath the warm remaining ashes, and got it going. How it worked. Then I was proud of myself. I went to the cooker and put a small piece of wood or big firewood and paper and was about to light it when my Mama came and really had a shock. Flames were coming out all over the place. It looked like I had started a great fire. I don't remember being told off, but my Papa surely didn't give me one of his smiles that morning.

CHAPTER 2: JACQUES' WRITINGS: VILLEHERVIERS, LOIRE VALLEY, 1941-1945

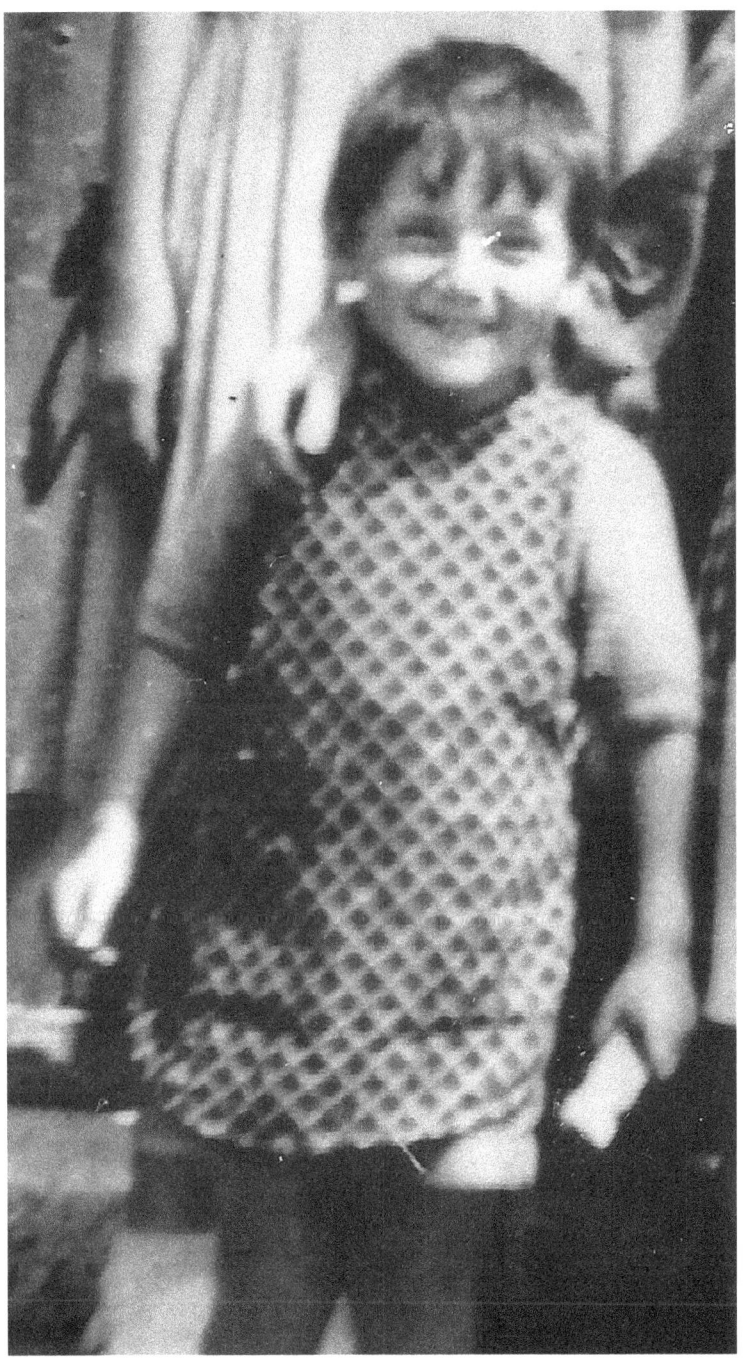

Jacques 1941/2

Play

My big brother and me, we used to go out early in the morning playing hide and seek towards the Railway Station. In early winter the *fog* would be so crushed against the trees that at times it would produce a little *hut* out of fog, and we would play in them and then on we would go, waiting for the train to go by, one daily. We would play by the lake on the way back. On the south end of the line was the Church where we used to go every Sunday. In the winter the lake would be frozen and tempting. I wasn't allowed on it.

Villeherviers

My red-haired brother used to go in the forest by himself, and sometimes he would come back with a rabbit – or animal red and yellow underneath. I think later that summer I went with my big brother rabbit hunting. He had one of those big sticks in his hand, over the hill plane we reached, poking in the hole, then waiting a minute or two, then it would come

CHAPTER 2: JACQUES' WRITINGS: VILLEHERVIERS, LOIRE VALLEY, 1941-1945

out, and he would hit the poor fellow with an accurate blow. Our dog we had was lazy as I remember he didn't do much walking, but he was one of us, the family. If it was fair weather outside, they would go to the lake that was iced over and skate. Everybody would feel relieved when cold was over – to me it didn't make any difference. I felt secure and happy. I recall one day we went out together with the goats. Since it was a very hot day, we stripped naked, then laid in the sun, not knowing that nearby was a beehive. Did we get stung and beaten up by them? We came back with bumps all over the place. Amazingly, it did not put me off bees. I knew next time to be careful, trial and error being my motto, although sometimes it doesn't matter.

As always, I was ahead of my family and suddenly I came upon a black and red thing, picking it up like it was a stick. It had a very pretty colour. Everybody stopped and said in a very polite way that I should just put it down because it was a nasty thing. As I put it down, it went on its way (that is one I wouldn't repeat today). It's so good when you don't have any fear. Everything seems so peaceful. The snake disappeared and that was the last time I ever saw such a beautiful snake or touched one. Except when I was at boarding school there was a chap there that had a grass snake, curled around his wrist.

> *Child category is pretty stick, adult category is dangerous snake. One trial learning here! Triggers other snake memories.*

In the Loire, on Saturdays we used to go to the motion pictures. If there were people in front that blocked the view, my brother would say I 'lost my snake', and everybody in front would run for their life. Those were happy times; I had not known that they were limited by days, minutes, seconds. A ten-year war of conflict was coming towards me

Evening meal, Papa and Mama
The evening meal was laid on the table with the supper and the cold wind raging outside. After supper we would move to the fireplace and

sit there watching the flames; it's crackling noise. It was a very quiet family. I never heard my parents yell – or even lose their temper at all. Our father, when he felt like it, would bring out his harmonica and play a tune. Do I remember them, their faces? But they were very kind people of good nature and thoughtfulness for the very few years that I had to spend there.

My mother used to go behind the house with me and pee – you see, I can do it standing up too. The first time it happened I was amazed because it didn't come into my mind that it was a very important thing that we must do.

Rhythm of Events

Harvest
Some time on the following day (after my arrival), I was taken out to the bright landscape where we stayed all day picking *grapes*. Well, they did. I was too busy fooling about and looking at the *house*. They filled the wagon full of grapes in time for pressing it with their feet. What zeal those guys had; and in the evening, we would travel back to the farm, and it was a rare thing for us to be awake when we arrived. I would wake up in the morning playing my role with Mama, crossing myself a couple of times for the good religion, then fooling around.

It was grape picking again and my parents would take off to the fields to do the picking and the rest of us went to school. On our way back we would go and do some of the picking ourselves. As usual I would help in the transport and on the wagon. Once it was filled it would be taken where they had this gigantic barrel. In the barrel there were four or five barefoot men walking on the grapes. When they finished of an evening, they would come laughing, saying they never had cleaner feet in their life. At the bottom of the barrel was a wooden tap. They got a glass and tasted the juice; it was a very sweet drink. Once they had it full, this would be a feast which everyone around the world would come and have the time of our life. Then when harvest came, my Papa would put all his grain in the loft; it was busy till the winter. The apples were very large in size; they would be all put in a large room on the floor of the outside room.

Christmas
Everybody looked at me as though I was supposed to doze off after that meal. Christmas came again and I decided that this year I would stay awake all night for Father Christmas, whatever happens. They all sat there talking near the fireplace and I laid there wide awake. As the time passed, I began to see things like if there were coats hanging on the back of the doors in a dark corner. I thought there were suddenly more people in that room than we started with. They were moving about my brain. I was looking at it, but I knew it couldn't be so, as I forced myself to keep awake.

> *Interesting that even at that early age Jacques only believed in 'real' people. No surprise he did NOT manage to stay awake. I came to know that when he was ready to sleep, he slept – thunderstorms and all.*

Then I woke up and dressed myself; it was my morning routine for the day. I went to the fireplace and went to see what Father Christmas brought me.

> *Frustrating not to know what Father Christmas DID bring, especially as he later says there were no toys.*

Sundays
On Sunday we would walk to the church and be quiet for a bit of praying. The inside was very dark and warm. One would not know really whether it was the cost of light that was expensive – but in those days I didn't even know that electricity existed, or car motors – only the cart wagon pulled by the horse – and of course the train. I mustn't forget the train.

Maverick: A memoir of Jacques Kornbrot, 1938 - 2014

What did he think he was praying about, and who to? Did he have any concept of God or Jesus? Did he have any idea WHY Mama crossed him every morning?

Easter
Easter came. Mama would make eggs boiled in onion peel and they would come out a brown colour and we would take off to the forest and have a full picnic bag the whole day. It was loaded with all kinds of berries and mushrooms, and we would pick them. Then there were some that you would put in hot water, and we would drink it while we were coming back on the track.

School, almost certainly 1944, just before his sixth birthday
The final day arrived, and I started school with hundreds of other boys of my age.

School is 6km walk

CHAPTER 2: JACQUES' WRITINGS: VILLEHERVIERS, LOIRE VALLEY, 1941-1945

The first thing that happened when I got there was that I got into a furious fight with another boy – and I threw my arms out like a bear, closing my eyes tight, moving from left to right, then we rolled on the ground. All the other kids were cheering away like a bunch of idiots. Once the fight was over, I had ripped my bottom and the underneath of my trouser and I looked like a little girl with a dress. On my way home I sat on a pile of sand that was warm from the afternoon sun. It felt good – as usual my Mama cuddled me, and I told her what happened, the whole truth, nothing but the truth.

Typical. Not naturally violent, he never saw the point. BUT he could certainly defend himself when necessary.

Germans and the Maquis

Prelude
Boom, and there was fire. It was like magic for many days to come. I would watch until I found out how he did this. He then had a breakfast and took off to the woods with the dog. I followed for a while, then came back to the farmhouse. I never did find out why he went into the woods. Although it was WW2 at the time, I didn't know, but on a winter's day my father put me on a bench and then shaved my hair off my head. Boy was I cold.

Arrival of Germans
Then somebody dropped in, and the conversation was very frightening. I didn't understand, but the atmosphere was worrying. My mother and sisters were preparing a meal and we were one more – my big brother was kidding around when all of a sudden there was a minute of silence, and the roaring of machines were heard, and our guest ran to the back of the house automatically. My mother took a plate off the table.

According to records at Blois, the Germans had a commander stationed in Romarantin by June 1940. But there was no sign of

25

Germans when Jacques arrived at the farm, at the earliest in summer 1941. Apparently the Luftwaffe used Romarantin as an aircraft park in 1940, but by the end of 1941 this activity had been moved elsewhere and the airfield was nearly deserted. So, it would make sense for Germans to arrive back at Villeherviers around 1943.

Then one afternoon from nowhere appear two vans and they were loaded with men in the same uniform, and they walked all about, talking a very, very weird language. As they walked past, they looked at me and I did not understand them to this day.

Then a truck stopped, uniformed people got out and they were like mumbling away. I could not understand; neither could my parents. I can't think what they were trying to tell me. There was fear in my parents' eyes as I kept very quiet and stared. One started to stutter. I felt like laughing because he looked like he was in pain, while the rest moved around without speaking. Our dog sniffed; he even got patted. Then one of them came up to me and smiled and gave me money and walked off. We saw them leave and went back inside; the guest came out of where he was hidden and took some cheese and bread, saying good boy. That was my first account between the goodies and the baddies. Who were the goodies and the baddies? My father was nervous at the uniform soldiers he met; they were not the goodies. Still, I didn't understand the situation.

French resistance
Although there was a war on, it was very peaceful. The French resistance used to drop by from time to time; they were very tall fellows and had black leather coats and serious most of them. They had converted one car into a half-track and another car into a small arms carrier. Some of those shaped up cars were very amusing, with gas tank on the roof – they even had some that ran on coal with a big chimney.

They would stop, and my father looked more happy with them than with the soldiers. It took me quite a while to understand the situation between the goodies and baddies. The baddies were much better dressed than the goodies. The goodies were always asked inside, for drink and food. The baddies always had to ask, and they paid in the end peacefully. Yet they were always coming around checking and asking questions. I was never told to say anything as people know children don't know anything. Well, there were a lot of people didn't want to know.

Parents' reactions and interactions with Germans

I cannot remember any bad time, even that they fed me the wrong information. My foster mother would say, 'If you're dirty, you're bad; if you're clean, you're good.' Well, when the Germans turned up, clean spit and shine, they disapproved, and everybody around was shit scared. I did not know what the fears were, just they were not happy about them, or the situation. But when the freedom fighters turned up, dirty, unshaven, like they had never washed for a million years, and these guys were welcomed with joy. It got quite confusing. It took me a long time to understand the situation I was in and who were the good guys, and who were the bad guys. Even that the Germans in my eyes were kinder, giving me things.

Resistance fighter, members of Maquis 1944

How to tell between what is a lie? Or just stories of lies for interest. If you tell the story you have got to add spices to it – no one likes to hear boring stories, especially me.

When the baddies came in to ask to have a meal or even stop to talk with him, so things around weren't the same. One day a German soldier turned up and said he wanted to have fried eggs. Mama started to make them sunny side up, but he wanted them flipped over, so she flipped them. I could see that Papa was really annoyed, and when he left, Papa said 'I could have finished him', but down deep inside he was too good a man to do it. The war continued. One day we would have spies, another the Maquis.

Another example of Jacques seeing self-control

One evening my father came home cursing and hating the baddies and saying they have killed the dog – they said he was a mutt at that. Papa buried the poor thing. From that time on my father was really furious; he would say, 'I should have killed one for the dog.'

Christmas and Germans
Since it was Christmas Day, we had a big lunch and there was a toy. Then there was an extra person that arrived, and he sat down with us and ate until everybody got up and the guest disappeared in the back room where we used to store the cheese, and his plate was removed and they all sat down again. Not before long we heard a lot of soldiers walk all over the place. They searched everywhere and asked questions of all of us or they just looked. It was short and quick, and they got back on their trucks and took off. It became a regular affair, them turning up. It was a game of hide and seek

The food stores were vanishing rapidly in the winter. People would go out hunting and come back with some of the weirdest creatures anyone has ever seen.

Yet he does not remember being hungry.

Germans at war end

The Second World War was coming to an end. My Papa was talking with a soldier about a bomb that was so great that it could blow off hundreds of feet under your feet. Then winter comes – and life returns to normal, and slowly those well-dressed German soldiers turn up in dirty clothes and were so damaged that they have lost everything and become the prisoners of France. In vague detail they still had a smile on their faces as they walked not far from us.

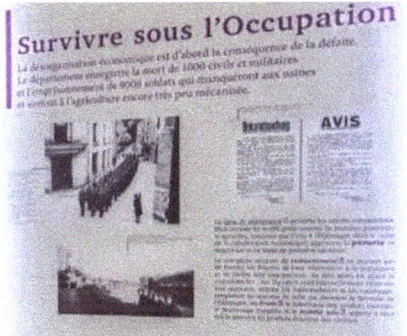

World War 2 ends

Reflecting on Villeherviers life.

Yes, I have crossed loads of frontier religions and all for the sake of living. This story that took place was one of a hundred thousand of children like me, that after the Second World War were reunited with the remains of their family. Of course, it was a disaster for me. I can't talk for the others, but that's the truth, and anyone that knows me from the time of 1945 till 1956 was one big disaster will recognise it.

Yes, from that little farm and my little world of theatres I was heading towards the greatest misery that I have ever received. What crime was committed against me is beyond any of today's dreams – and over time it still continues. I see what is right and wrong as it was in my life and that is honest.

Not to forget we were involved with the Second World War. What if the story about the aftermath had been different? Later, I look back at it and wonder if I would have been different if my father would have lived and my mother wouldn't have recovered from her illness mentally.

Yearnings: Up to finding Denise, Jacques' foster sister

If I could even see a photograph of that place just a moment. It is so sad that I was taken away from that quiet lovely farmhouse where peace was in me two hundred percent, hour and hour. Unjust. But at that age one's point of view wasn't asked for; you just had to accept. I would've remembered things much more clearly today. Alas, it's not as if I have tried very hard to find that little place out there, one side of me wanting very much to find it and the other side just to remember it as it was put there in my mind. If only I could find that place now. I know my parents would have passed away, but my red-haired brother and my two sisters must still be living somewhere, somewhere in France.

It was so nice finding my sister was not far away from where we all lived during the war.

> Jacques finally found Villeherviers by visiting his old primary school in Paris, where they had records of his previous school! Reunion was dramatic.

A happy childhood

But let me go back when I was a happy child with no worry or cares. It was a good, pleasant life, but with no light except for candles to keep the house alight. It was a very quiet farm except for the animals and those who would pass by on the road in a buggy. My foster parents, who at the time I truly thought were my parents, cared about me like they should. Although my Papa, in the corner of his eyes at time, would've liked to beat the hell out of me. Yet he remained strong and kept his hand to himself. I don't remember at all anybody hitting me or yelling.

Jacques observed a good example of someone tempted to hit out but controlling himself. It made a lifelong impression that he always followed. All his memories are of feeling happy and living with good people.

CHAPTER 3.
CHILDHOOD, 1945-1951

The Second World War had ended. The planet was picking up the pieces. History and myths about the roles of nations and individuals were created. No more genocide, peace on earth, the USSR was our gallant ally, they all said. Well, not Churchill; he gave his Iron Curtain speech in 1946.

In France, for Jacques this spelled total disaster. He reflected it was probably a disaster for many displaced kids. Later, he mused about how his life might have been different if his father had survived.

Diana learnt just what had happened to her great-grandfather and many of her cousins. Jacques learnt his 'real' father was murdered. In the UK, Diana perceived it as a time of optimism.

Jacques' transition, Paris, 1945-1951

Transition
Jacques had no idea his mother was in an asylum. He thought her not visiting him during the Second World War was by choice. He contrasted this with the mother of his friend Emanuel, who managed to visit her two sons in Belgium from Paris with much difficulty.

First meeting with his mother
Jacques was totally bewildered. His mother made a visit in late autumn 1945, having been released from the asylum into the care of her nephew in October 1945. She came alone. Jacques was told that she was his mother. He was instantly repelled. Up until then he had assumed the foster parents were his real parents. He does not seem to have wondered why he met them for the first time in a hospital. He was a practical child,

dubious about Father Christmas. He can't have believed people came into this world on a hospital bed confronted by a big fish. He must have seen babies around the place.

His foster parents then gave up their bedroom to a reunion between Jacques and his mother. She tried to suckle him. He was appalled and completely rejected and hated her. Not an auspicious start. Jacques was confused and horrified, but she left the next day and life returned to 'normal' and he vainly hoped never to see her again.

From Villeherviers to Paris
Later, in 1945 or early 1946, social workers came to collect him. He was taken to an orphanage/hospital, with no explanation of what was happening or why. He was scrubbed within an inch of his life and sent to a playground with children, and even adults, in various degrees of normal playfulness and extreme distress. Some had been liberated from concentration camps. This short experience of institution life was dramatic. It probably influenced his later unwillingness to protest to authorities about his mother. He knew even worse things were possible.

Paris
Jacques was returned to his mother, who was living with her nephew Jacques (the son of a brother who died during the war – according to the asylum, a 'natural' death in hospital with no explanation of what happened to his wife). BUT, according to his cousin Jacques' story, his parents were killed by Germans while he was hiding in the toilet.

Jacques got on fine with his cousin, who helped him with schoolwork. He must have been an engaging, outgoing kid who easily made friends – except with his mother. He caught his mother and cousin Jacques *in flagrante*. He registered disapproval by crashing plates to the kitchen floor. They stopped. He remained on good terms with his cousin.

CHAPTER 3: PRIMARY SCHOOL YEARS, 1945-1948

Rebellion, friendly police

Jacques hated every minute of his Paris life and started to become a rebel and an outsider. He ran away as often as he could. He became quite an expert. The police were happy to play with him and give him sandwiches, but in the end he was, of course, returned to his mother. She punished him physically to an extent we would now call child abuse.

School and religion, conflicting identity, and mores

Jacques went to school in Paris, but doesn't mention any particular friends, or being singled out for good or bad behaviour or performance. He did fight a lot, but still could not see any point other than standing up for himself. He was introduced to the synagogue in the women's gallery. He did not see the point of attending the service, with seemingly ugly men in funny costumes mumbling in an incomprehensible language. His mother proudly declared these were 'our people'. But to Jacques, his people were back in the village, in the home he always hoped to return to.

Role of social services

There was no check on his mother's mental health or Jacques' welfare. He was registered as a French citizen by right of birth. His mother remained an alien. So, to get a passport to emigrate to Australia, social services approval was required. They *did* ask 10-year-old Jacques if he wanted to go. He stayed shtum. He had spent a week in an orphanage/institution and could imagine worse things even than his mother.

Diana, 1945-1951: London, 'real' school

London

Life was returning to normal. My family were growing up and aspiring to independence. I learned to ride a bicycle received on my sixth birthday, and still have motor memories of the wonderful moment when Dad let go and hurrah, I got to the end of the garden solo.

My first real friendship was with Juliet, throughout school years and sporadically after. Peers became an important influence; at the time, they seemed much more important than parents, teachers, or religious education. In retrospect, who knows.

Memorable travel

In alternate years we spent time in English rented seaside houses, e.g. Kingsgate, and abroad. In 1947, it was Denmark: memorable castles, long days on the beach, no restrictions on food. I even saw a man feed an ice cream to a *dog*! It was fascinating to see cars loaded onto a ship by crane. We had a puncture on the way back to Esbjerg port, and friends persuaded the captain to wait. Travel was another dimension then. This holiday must have reminded Edmonde and Harry of their last holiday before the war, when I was conceived, and similarly another new life was started, Myke.

Myke arrives 21st May 1948

What excitement! Mother was in hospital. We all discussed names round the ritual Saturday dinner table with Dad and grandparents. I had little interest in baby Myke; Tim was more interested. Myke became interesting as he grew up and could put his oar in any conversation. I got ever closer as we grew up. Now Myke is a key element of my life, as he was also for Jacques.

Diana & brothers Tim, Myke

Science, religion, conflicting identity, and mores

From age six, at least, onwards, I wanted to be a scientist and know how the physical world worked. Feelings of being 'different' continued throughout childhood, and is there, basically the same, in my eighties. At 11, given the choice, I chose to stay at progressive mixed school, King Alfred School, rather than an academic hot house girls' school.

There was conflict for me between school mores – outwardly despising material goods, especially clothes – and home mores, where special clothes for Saturdays and Jewish holidays were mandatory (and uncomfortable). I dreaded being seen in them by school mates. I knew I was considered 'brainy', and good at maths, but not that good at games or writing or art. I mistakenly believed there was some equity so that being good at one thing was compensated by being bad at other things. This was flagrantly contradicted by experience. Clearly, not a view based on 'evidence'. Juliet, for example, was *very* good at everything except music; Joyce/Riva at everything except sports.

Friends at wedding 1973
Faustin, Dalia, Jo, Juliet Jacques, Diana, Francis, Juliet's mother, Joyce/Riva

I took being both Jewish and English for granted. I assumed that anti-Semitism had been finally conquered by the horrors of the Holocaust. This was up to 11 years old, but how many 'ethnic minority' kids get to 11 years old without being aware of racism these days, in England or France? In the UK, Jewish schools and synagogues now have security guards. This was written before the October 2023 Israeli-Hamas events. Anti-Semitism increased around 10-fold and Islamophobia about two-fold.

Comparison of experiences: Jacques' and mine
Jacques suffered disastrous unloved primary school years from seven through 10 in France. He survived in the face of people trying to convince him he was 'bad'. By contrast, I had an expanding, interesting, normal, loving primary school time from five to 11, living in comfortable suburbia.

Diana's childhood home

Nevertheless, I also had conflicts between different social milieus – home, school, Judaism. I also felt an outsider. Feeling an outsider was something we shared and was part of our growing up. For many, growing up may reinforce attachment to communities of one sort or another. Not for us

CHAPTER 4.
JACQUES' WRITINGS, 1945-1951

Transition to Paris

First contact with mother, winter 1945

One winter day, as I walked out of the house, I saw my foster papa with this woman, and they talked. She turned up in the forestry house at the edge of the woods that I always thought to be a farmhouse because of all the animals we had. It must have been near Christmas when she turned up, as there was snow on the ground covering the whole of the area.

She stood in the courtyard. Then I was introduced to her as my real mother. After seven years, this woman turned up from nowhere – I looked at my foster parents in amazement. I started to question everybody.

The first meeting must have been winter 1945. He had no idea of her existence.

My second war was about to start. I did not know at the time that the way ahead would last 10 troubling years. But, as with any nation, I made my revolution at an early age and haven't much changed that pattern.

We all sat down to have a meal and me going, 'Oui, madame', 'Oui, monsieur', etc. What polite talk. I didn't know whether I was coming or going. After the meal, I was taken to the room where usually my foster parents slept, and I was put in bed. A minute later my real mother, the woman that God brought to me, got into bed with me. She just talked to me and then cuddled me, and I felt dreadful – and then she wanted to suckle me! I was horrified. It was disgusting. I moved away in a panic.

Maverick: A memoir of Jacques Kornbrot, 1938 - 2014

Whether I yelled I don't remember, with what little French I had, but she let me go.

I hated her; nor did I understand the meaning of what she was doing. When I think that at birth she rejected me – and wouldn't open her eyes or act for a year. She waited seven years until the Second World War was over, but that's another story. I guess that must have triggered something in my child brain or mind, a resentment shift when I think of it. This woman from nowhere fell asleep and in the morning she left. I was hoping to never see her again. What a dirty night.

> *Jacques never knew that his mother had been sectioned in an asylum since before the war (January 1939) until July 1945, well after the liberation of Paris. He only knew that she was too mentally ill to care for him and would not open her eyes. I only knew of her stay in the asylum after Jacques' death.*

She went towards the station and that was that, like nothing happened. I went back to calling my foster parents Mama and Papa – for a while.

Torn from Villeherviers. The end of a happy childhood

Then a couple came to take me away. A suitcase was ready, and I felt at the time like one of the photographs in *The World at War*, over the picture of a child looking bewildered at what was happening. There was no sadness at the time; everybody acted like I was going on a picnic, and they had a small basket of food to take with me.

> *Jacques told me a story of running away and hiding because he knew his mother was bad news. It took the family a whole day to find him.*

It was the closing of my youth at the age of eight, standing at the door of the farmhouse, that I remember so well. I felt lost, like just before going to battle, not knowing if I shall ever return to my origin.

If he was eight, then it was after October 1946. It is not clear how long a period separated his first meeting with his mother and his journey to Paris. He may have misremembered eight and he was actually seven in winter of 1945.

Journey to Paris

I didn't think my foster parents came to the train. It must have been a very sad moment in their life losing me; like I had more in common with them than I had with that woman – 'mother', as I must call her.

The social welfare, I presume, took me off to the train, and without saying much we arrived in Paris. The train journey was long, and I ate twice – their faces and eyes watched. Those foods were so strange, and I didn't even eat; I swallowed, and it gave me a feeling like choking oneself. I think we changed trains. We arrived in Paris late in the night, and the station wasn't like the one we had near the farm. There were many buildings in different sizes and shapes – it looked quite interesting.

Childhood end

The freedom that I had around the farm and forest was shortly to be ended by closed doors and mental violence. My childhood stopped at that moment. My first stop was the hospital, where I stayed for a week among the sick, and probably some ex-prisoners.

Hospital/orphanage

Hospital was frightening. There were many people there with a pipe leading from the bed. It was frightening because so far no one bothered to tell me really why I was to be there in the first place.

I had my first bath, in a very big bathtub. The nurse was very young, and she scrubbed me like I was never scrubbed in my life. I came out all red. *Voila*, one cleaned, scrubbed boy. Since that day, I never had a bath like that.

I had breakfast and was taken out to where the hospital had this very large courtyard. Within it there were many children of all ages. Some of them were laughing and playing; others were in corners with fear written all over their faces. Later, I heard that it was children who were just coming back from concentration camps. There was a man that was very strange; one small child would come to him and raise his hand. He would yell back, 'Don't, don't hurt me!' I couldn't believe my eyes. I even followed suit, and then he went yelling, 'Don't, don't!' That hospital was scary. This was not Villeherviers. The experience is vivid like it was today. Today, now it is still happening somewhere, and all we can say is, 'Those poor people.'

Hospital days

The couple of days I was there were not pleasant ones really. A male nurse would go around giving everybody injections. I must admit I never received any, but it was frightening because no one there liked it; they didn't smile. Some of them had sore throats and the nurse would come out with a short stick with cotton at the end and a purple colour. Then she would say, 'Who has a sore throat?', and some of them would say, 'Me.' They would open their mouths and with this stick she would poke it in. I said to myself, even if I have a sore throat, I would never let anybody do that to me. That evening, the nurse came to me and I thought, 'This is it, she is going to take me for another bath.' No, she was just checking on me.

Disaster: transfer to mother

Then I was dressed up again with my clothes, and the greatest disaster of my life turned up: my mother, my Yiddish mother. How they ever gave them this name is beyond me. I should really be anti-Jewish after what I was going to go through. They took me to an office, and there was that woman that was supposed to be my mother. She came over and kissed me, saying she was going to take me home. Well, I was happy. I thought, 'Good, off to the farm again.'

What a disaster. What a crime was committed, but no one really wants to know, as long as they don't have the responsibility on their hands. Maybe if I would have yelled, kicked and rejected her from the start, things might have been different. But I come from a house that was peaceful, there was no bitter or ill feeling about anything that I can remember. Yelling was not my foster parents' way. It was a very peaceful home at that.

In the short period being with my mother's bitterness, she failed to understand that she was supposed to be a mother. She was more an incapable human being, always saying that it was someone else's fault. For her points were easy to read, but one could not really learn anything much but the bitterness that she was in. As far as I understand, she came from a middle-class, educated family, and yet was a moron. I come back to the thing of her not doing the right things. She did things like today what pleased her and not what really should be done about this very delicate situation. She was great at punishing things, like, 'You did a bad thing and because you did it you are not going to the pictures.

Paris

The great city, first impression
As we left the hospital into the street, I was confronted with tall buildings in a high and very impressive way; no trees or forest, but people, lots of people. As we walked down the road, we came to stairs that led underground; it was the Métro. We travelled for a bit and got off and back to the light of the day and saw those big houses, and we entered one of them and walked up a flight of stairs.

Maverick: A memoir of Jacques Kornbrot, 1938 - 2014

Jacques & Mother, Paris 1946

Cousin Jacques

She opened the door, and I was introduced to my cousin Jacques. She lived on the 6th floor with him. He was in his early 20s and had lost his parents. I don't know if this is true, but they say that when the Germans came to take them away, he was in the toilet, and they killed his parents in bed because they did not want to go. He went into hiding.

> *The asylum records have a story that Marie's brother (cousin Jacques' father) died in hospital, but there is no mention of a mother. Who knows what the Germans chose to tell the asylum?*

Whatever, I got along with him much better than my mother. My mother was always full of complaining about anything you could mention. She made me feel guilty about everything and anything. She was a taker, not a giver. Even going to the 6th floor was hard for her. Because of me she couldn't marry again, although she met a lot of men; even then she still complained about it. I really don't remember any good times. Everything was just bad, and the worst of things was to come. She really was not made to be a mother. Until this day she still complained. There I was in one big flat on the 6th floor, locked in, and all I could do was to look and wave at an old lady across the street.

- Then I knew I would never see that farm again, or my foster parents.

His desolation is unimaginable.

In flagrante
One of those famous evenings after supper I was told to do the dishes and then went into my cousin's place and started with the dishes. My curiosity was alerted. I went in and before my eyes I saw my cousin pushing my mother against the wall, with my mother making soft breathing noises. She looked like she was enjoying herself and they were making love. Without blinking my eyelids, I went back to the kitchen and picked up a pile of plates and dropped them. What a noise! In a split second, they came in and saw what happened – and had the coffee spilled all over the place, the chair, and the cup on the ground. So then she sprang on me. 'Because you did it, you are not going to the pictures.' It was one of the first events that I saw her comment, 'What would the Christians say?'

Comparing foster family and life with mother
From a big family I had come down to one woman and my cousin Jacques, as they say. At the time I was in the flat, there was a soft man. When I started to go to school, he would help me with the work – he was making a fur coat at the time, cutting pieces and sewing them together. Then he would fill the bath with water and stretch it out on a big board to dry.

Social life, growing dissatisfaction
Yes, the honeymoon, as the politicians today call it, was probably one or two days, for after that it was one big chaos. My dissatisfaction grew

slowly, but it grew and grew. She never did tell me about my father, except that he was killed in a camp. She didn't tell me that it was Auschwitz.

So brave, so tough. I cry for him every time I read this.

Learning about Jewishness

I was just back in time when I was told I was Jewish. She took me to the synagogue, and we sat in the balcony. The first thing I did was to take off my cap – and then she put it back on again and she said that I was Jewish and that the men don't take off their hats for God. Around me there were only small boys and girls and women up in that balcony.

What weird stuff. Looking down, I saw these bearded men – ugly things and frightening, looking evil – and then they were waving their bodies, hard about front, backwards, sidewards, putting their hands over their faces; and none of them had a happy look in their eyes.

My mother kept repeating with sparkling eyes, 'These are our own people.' What was I supposed to answer? She felt proud of being Jewish. She told me that the Germans were very hard people, and it seemed that it fitted poorly into my little brain. It looked to me that the synagogue people looked a meaner lot than the Germans. I was in a daze. So, these were my new people. I knew I didn't like it, as we walked back to the 6th floor flat.

The dentist

The next day we went to the dentist. It was a frightening experience. One of my little teeth had grown over the other, and he took something that looked like a tool, pushing the tooth in. Out came the tooth, but it was too late. I nearly fainted. I felt like I was being punished.

Social life with mother

She took me around, showing me off to everybody, but there was more sadness than happy ones. When I was bad, she would yell at me – and say, 'If you don't change your attitude, a bogey man in black will come and take you away.' Then, one night, she got herself picked up by a black man – he took us to eat, and she had an affair in the movie house, and I thought, 'Good, she is going to be taken away by the black bogey man.' No, she was not. He walked us most of the way home and we never saw him again – there was still a lot that I had to understand in the position I was in. Many things happened, too strange for words.

Maturing

I used to wake up screaming. Maybe it was the idea of the bogey man taking me away. Why was I revolting around her? Why was I unable to explain myself or tell you why I lied to force her to become understandable?

Unimaginable, a child screaming with no one to comfort him.

Slowly, I was maturing, becoming more involved in my forced life of Paris. When there were school holidays, I was locked in for days on end. I heard of the baby stories that didn't exist in my little world. The whole structure that was put in front of me disappeared. It was not a game anymore.

Jacques 1946, aged 8

When I was let out, I would rush off to a church that was a hundred times bigger than the one I used to go to. The door would always be wide open, but not a soul was there, and the fountain of holy water was big – I used to put my little hands in it and bathe them. I think there was no chance of me going to where people stay for talk.

The idea of prayer does not seem to have occurred to him despite his dire situation, and his apparent Catholic upbringing. But he got some comfort form the church.

Rebellion

Slowly, I became wilder and wilder; no one had any control over me. The boredom made me revolt the more. As I think back to my foster parents, who knows what would have happened if they had left me with them.

I started to revolt. I even tried to run away. I walked around for a long time and I got lost in Paris and ended up in a police station, eating somebody's lunch. I spent quite a long time with them. They played around with me and gave me chocolate, we sang songs, and it was a very happy moment. Then that mother came to take me home. I had finally started my new career of running away.

He was so engaging, everyone wanted to play with him, given the chance, and so he remained until his death.

Punishment

After that I was locked in like a dog on the 6th floor when she left to work or out in the evening to meet with her lover. She never realised the fact that I didn't care whether she lived or died. As for me, it didn't make any difference to me. She was just a very selfish person with no intention of being a mother. There I was in one big flat on the 6th floor, locked in, and all I could do was to look and wave at an old lady across the street.

CHAPTER 4: JACQUES' WRITINGS: TRANSITION AND PARIS, 1945-1948

Need for love
What I needed at the time was love, lots of love and caring; but I didn't get what I wanted. What I got was, as she would say at me, 'Because of you I can't re-marry.' I couldn't get over it; home was a nightmare. There was nothing there for me except this woman who was forcing me to be a grown-up at an early age. 'You are the grown-up.' I wonder how I must have meditated into space, not knowing that I needed a family life, an area of joy intended. My environment was slowly changing what I had of my youth. I compare the childhoods of others I know which are more normal than me and had laughter. Laughter was minimal for me.

School
Then I started to go to school. The only good thing was that I didn't have to walk seven kilometres there and back. I went every morning in the gigantic build of Paris – in the classroom that was so large compared to the one I went to near the farm, with the open view and the green fields. I COULDN'T GET USED TO IT.

I stayed there two years before we left for Australia. My school days were nice. I got out to play and got into fights. I used to come home with a bloody nose and black eyes – when one was healing, the other one got punched in. I surely didn't protect my face properly. I became a real militant little fellow.

Transition to Australia
Since my mother was not French, the social welfare, or somebody from the French government, asked if I wanted to go and if she was a good person. What could I say, knowing that if I said it was bad, I would probably be sent to a worse place than there? Alas, it would not have mattered. There was still worse to come. The goodness that I have in me is not from my Jewish blood, but from that elderly couple that were foster parents that knew how to be real parents. In their lifespan they had fostered 45

children. They were so good that they were given something like the Legion d'Honneur

CHAPTER 5
LATER CHILDHOOD 1948-1958

The Cold War was by now well established. Western Europe was coming to terms with what *really* happened in Eastern Europe under Stalin. The American Far East policy embraced the Korean War, supported by the British (Labour and Conservative) and by Australia, while its South American policy supported dictators and luxury organised crime. The Europeans were making last ditch attempts to save their empires. India, Pakistan (1947) and Israel (1948) became independent of the UK with much blood loss. The French were losing disastrously in Indochina, laying the foundations for the Vietnam War.

Jacques: Australia, 1948-1956

Jacques' Australian experiences are even more harrowing than his French ones, because he is much more aware of what he is missing: not just the loving family on the farm, but also an education with opportunities and people around who valued him and saw his potential.

His writings come back time and again to what *could* have been done and what actually happened. He recognises the good intentions of family, the indifference of teachers and schools, and psychologists and psychiatrists, focussed on how his behaviour affected the welfare of his mother, not at all on *his* problems. He describes his need for love and at least one sympathetic adult and on what might have been achieved with just one month of language instruction contrasted with near useless psychological interviews. General reflections arising from Australian events are in chapter 10.

He describes his arrival in Australia and events in three radically different environments: the home front with an incompetent and sometimes seriously depressed mother and a well-meaning but uncomprehending family; Ballarat a private school in the country; and the Melbourne street environment with Carlton street gangs and Joe's Café a haunt of other outsiders and petty criminals.

Arrival in Australia
Planning had involved painful inoculations necessitating days in bed. The voyage was by aeroplane via India, and, typically, with minimum explanation of what was going on. Landfall was Sydney.

Meeting the family
The Melbourne family was large and constituted not only his mother's brothers and sister (Aunt Rose), but also his mother's cousin, Norman Rockman, who was a wealthy, influential Melbourne businessman. Jacques was taken to synagogues, where his bachelor uncle tried to make him 'a nice Jewish boy'.

Rockman family gathering 1948?

Of course, he did not speak any English and was also exposed to Hebrew at mealtimes and prayers in the home (a language he found 'harsh'). He was bewildered and had no one to turn to. The agony of separation from his original foster family in France was always in the background. Knowing a good family life made his dysfunctional Australian experience all the more harrowing.

Melbourne

Living conditions
The family seems to have supplied his mother with accommodation. In the first house, he still had to share a bed with her, which he obviously hated. Subsequently, they moved to a boarding house that his mother managed. The lodgers came from many different countries and had keys. Jacques also got a room to himself with a key.

Relations with his mother
His rebellion, started in France, escalated. His mother beat him and tried to lock him in. He responded by running away and describes several incidents.

> *He told me that he once got half-way across Australia on a train.*

Primary school
He was sent to Princes Hill primary, while still having minimal English. He did not get good marks or make friendships. The teachers reported he 'could do better', as teachers do the world over. No one thought that the teachers or school 'could do better', e.g., English lessons. Corporal punishment was an integral part of school life. Very different from France, where teachers did not hit kids – ever, apparently.

So, he 'bunked off'. He jettisoned tasteless sandwiches supplied by his mother and snuck into the movies (probably with other kids).

Maverick: A memoir of Jacques Kornbrot, 1938 - 2014

Religion
His uncle took him to synagogue on Saturday. On Sundays, he was sent to religious school with yet more corporal punishment. Aunt Rose advised him to hit back. On the next occasion, he can't even remember whether he or another kid was hit, but he broke the teacher's jaw, and then left class in a hurry. He was not forced to return.

> *He later told me that a bar mitzvah was arranged, but he ran off on the way to synagogue. He is the only person I know who did not attend his own bar mitzvah.*

Summer camp
The family also tried sending him to a Jewish summer camp he called Burwood, possibly an offshoot of Mount Scopus Day School. He notes the unpleasant smell of unwashed boys and the incomprehensibility of the religious instruction. It lasted a week, but am not sure if that was the intention, or he simply took off.

Family holidays
Cousin Norman invited the whole family to summer seaside holidays. The family included Norman's three children, Jacques and his mother, and his mother's elder brother with grandchildren (Adele, same age as Jacques,

Melbourne Marina

Ian, now dead, and youngest Ray with whom we later became friends). Jacques enjoyed the freedom, swimming, and boating.

Family interventions and good intentions
As an adult, and maybe even as a child, he recognised that the family had good intentions. They were faced with a traumatised, but very articulate adult (the mother), who was still clearly mentally ill with depression, even if no longer psychotic. What Jacques longed for, but was unable to explain, was just one adult who would listen. He thought it should have been obvious: firstly, even one month of one-to-one English tuition would have made an enormous difference; and secondly that the running away must have been due to really bad problems at home.

The family had him assessed by numerous psychiatrists. These were as useless as the 'could do better' teachers. You need to *ask* a 10-year-old, why he is running away? The answer 'not happy at home', is hardly rocket science. Apparently, no attempt was made to change his mother's behaviour or help her understand Jacques' point of view via talking therapy of any kind, but she did receive drugs for depression.

After one of his long runaway episodes, there was a crisis family conference from which he was dispatched without delay to Ballarat, a private boarding school run on English public-school lines.

Ballarat School
He started at Ballarat Grammar in an age-appropriate class and was steadily put down a class each year. No one paid any attention to his lack of English, or even appear to have given him any individual attention. Ballarat was happy to receive the fees without giving a monkey's about a foreign kid's welfare. If Ballarat had suggested individual tutoring, the family would have been more than happy to pay. Of course, his school reports were 'could do better'. In my view, Ballarat's behaviour was ethically corrupt.

When he was with the younger boys, he became the defender of the bullied and a sort of 'judge'. Kids trusted him, all his life starting early. He did enjoy the countryside and became an excellent swimmer, after a nasty early shock. It illustrates his resilient ability to pick himself up and learn from any situation.

Carlton social and Joe's Café
Jacques' friend Willy Halpert remembers Carlton had a substantial Jewish community, with youths in the Hashomer Zionist group that Willy led and mentored. Through them, he met Jacques who laughed and told him about how he took the mickey out of the local tough guy in such a joking manner that the guy broke out in laughter and declared to all and sundry that Jacques was under his protection. Everybody in the area was then very polite with Jacques, which annoyed him. So, he did his routine with mocking exaggerated respect and regained his former friendships. Jacques was himself never a member of any gang or group. Willy and Jacques became casual friends then, and much closer after Eilat. Willy never took offence at Jacques' amusing teasing that persisted throughout his life. Willy still smiles remembering the surprised or shocked look of even strangers that inevitably turned into amused smiles.

When he was home for the holidays, or possibly even before, Jacques found a social group at Joe's Café. He became streetwise, but uninterested in criminal activity. He was fascinated by *everybody's* individual story.

Departure
After he left school, perhaps at 16, he had odd jobs, including as a postman, but nothing that excited him. He left or ran away. His story was that he was working on a Japanese merchant ship or maybe a tanker. Apparently his first destination was Morocco. However, he reached Israel from Greece, but his luggage was permanently lost – including his address book. It was the start of a new era.

Diana: England, 1945-1958

School and social life
I spent 1945-1956 at a progressive co-educational private school, King Alfred School, where I was very happy and made lifelong friendships. I was seen as 'brainy', good at maths and science, but not games or the arts. I wanted to be a physicist from age seven, or before. I was really interested in history, inspiringly taught by Marxist John Hanson, but saw no point in English essay or in poetry. That did not stop me getting absorbed in novels with action, historical, and contemporary, with *Wuthering Heights* a favourite – because of the passion. I thought Jane Austen was boring beyond belief and did not understand what my mother (with a degree in English) saw in her.

My last two years were at Queen's College, a private girls' school, where pupils were mainly doctors' daughters, often intending themselves to become doctors. Ethel Truman was a superb physics teacher. I was shortlisted for Cambridge, but failed the interview and extra tests. Some 60 years later, it occurred to me that anti-Semitism might have played a part. Certainly, the principal of the college was very cold, unforthcoming, and snooty. I was accepted at Bristol University. I was disappointed at the time, but am now extremely glad it worked out that way.

Religion
I attended Orthodox United Synagogue Hebrew classes at Norrice Lea and found learning history, classical Hebrew, and ancient laws fascinating. My parents were strong believers in the communal aspects of Judaism, but not the dietary or drive on Sabbath aspects. What did they believe spiritually? I do not know! Surprisingly few parents actually talked about their spiritual beliefs in those days, and probably still don't. The Ten Commandments came from a divine spiritual source? There was something out there to pray to who could affect life on earth? I suspect my father only believed in the communal, but I did not get to talk to him about it as he died too soon in 1966 at age 54. I did not really talk to my mother about

spiritual things either. All I knew was that it was important to support the Jewish community and Israel as a modern democratic state. Now I know that Israel is not *so* wholly democratic, in thrall to Haredi Judaism that represents a minuscule proportion of Israeli Jews. Israel denies full citizenship rights to women in terms of marriage and divorce, as well as to Israeli Arabs. Equal voting rights are necessary, but not sufficient for democracy. The Netanyahu government is planning to revoke Arab rights and independence of the Judiciary. Perhaps the October 2023 events will trigger a rethink, back to core democratic Zionist aspirations?

My grandfather Solomon was Orthodox, and I think he did believe in the spiritual side. My parents and grandparents strongly supported the democratic, socialist state of Israel, financially as well as emotionally. What would they have thought of Netanyahu and the many racists in the current state of Israel? Not at all what they had hoped and fought for. What would they have thought of their great grandson Richard becoming Haredi with all its misogynism and extremism? What would they have thought of my decision to NOT leave any money to Richard? We will never know because here on earth is all we have.

I was an atheist by age 12, if not before. I also hated attending synagogue: the clothes were uncomfortable, and it was so boring, and so hard to sit still , it still is. (I probably had undiagnosed ADHD; thankfully ADHD was not recognised in those days).

UK political situation
1945 was supposed to be the rise of a new dawn with equal opportunities for all, led by the landslide-elected Labour Government. Of course, the new Jerusalem was not built in a day, if at all, and citizens became fed up with rationing and restriction. What was achieved? The NHS, free education up to the age of 15 and many working class and non-professional children went to university: Joan Bakewell, Margaret Thatcher. Not in the same proportions as the wealthier and professional elite, but there all the same, and influential in the later 20th century. Palestine and the Indian

sub-continent became free from colonialism, but at a cost of much blood and bad feeling. In 1973, the UK was one of the most equal nations on the planet, in 2023 it is one of the most unequal among modern democracies (EU, North America, Australasia).

After the Second World War, many on the left were Soviet sympathisers, and some were outright communists. 1956 was a watershed; we got to know what *really* happened under Stalin. No, most people did NOT know; fake news and propaganda is not new. So, in 1956, I was in Trafalgar Square with classmates, demonstrating against the Soviet invasion of Hungary. There was a concurrent demo on the English and French invasion of the Suez Canal. Obviously, that was more difficult for me, as I did not want Israel swept into the sea, but disapproved of colonialism. Turns out Israelis did not need the colonial powers anyway! Heady times for a teenager.

CHAPTER 6
JACQUES' WRITINGS AUSTRALIA 1948-1956

France to Australia

A man that came with my mother – I thought, well here is another man to push her against the wall, well he wasn't. He asked if I wouldn't mind going away, I guess I nodded as usual – thought maybe I was going back, well it wasn't that. In our house I never knew anything, everything was secret here. They' were like people who are going to land a business deal.

After that we went to a hospital and queued up and it reminded me of the hospital where I had that nurse wash me down with a brush. It was painful, everybody was getting these long injections under the shoulder blade. It didn't look amusing at all one male nurse held you – saying "we have injections for you". We drove home and stayed in bed for a week with pain, it was enough, a touch and you would be screaming blue murder.

Then the final day came we were taken to the aircraft in the night and boarded a plane with hundreds of people. They frightened me. They all looked scared and passed it on to me. We were up in the air. I started to have a stomach-ache, and the stewardess came with a pill saying that if I don't have pain, it will not work. So, she put the fear of life in me, I didn't take it. The journey took quite a long time but that's another story. We arrived in Sydney in the night, and we could see the light flooding about like stars towards the promised land. I hardly heard French, to tell you the truth.

We were taken to a tea house and had the very thin sandwiches, and I finished the bunch in one go, everybody laughed. I didn't know that you had to eat them one by one and not like a French sandwich. We stayed in Sydney for quite a while and boarded another plane to Melbourne. Waiting for us was my uncle, and then I fell asleep.

The next four days we were taken around to meet all the family. There were quite a lot of them. The first Saturday I was taken with the man of the house. At every end of the prayer my uncle would take my chin in his hand and say Amen and repeated it time over and over. Then we went home and prayed again for the meal. I was starving, they such took a long time. Once having finished the meal they continued, in what to me was the longest time, in a language was horrible and sounded very aggressive. In the morning, I looked, and all around the round were the men one more ugly than the other. A completely different world was there, I saw. In the end, my uncle turned out to be a nice man and tried to make out of me a nice Jewish boy. The others included one nice old man, he was a great learner of the bible and spoke well. He was always talking, and everybody listened.

Separation: lives torn apart
How I longed to go back to Villeherviers with its woods and serenity. They couldn't have known it. It's painful today when I look back at this horrible moment of my youth that was destroyed in a single blow. Those few early years that I had made a lot of difference to my part of life.

> *Prayer apparently never occurred to him, although he got comfort form the church in Paris. The influence of childhood religious education is mysterious.*

Yes, I was taken to a foreign land, that wasn't made for me, or any child with my background. A child doesn't have to know these problems or even go through this movement of evil. It's only when he **is** old enough to select what is good for him. Yet he is not an individual, because he trained, from one involvement for another. I can truly own I missed my family on the Farm – among the trees the happiness I had then – it's the past and I have to control this. Yes, I was a boy from the countryside – the farm and my family. It's very hard for anybody to understand my side of this story as it follows finding out so many things that I am supposed to accept without question, being obedient my new state, like nothing ever happened. I was supposed to overnight accept the evil woman as my mother protector. I was supposed to go through a re-programming in the world of alien adults, after spending most of my very young childhood where my real person belonged to.

Man, I am lazy today. Everybody runs away from the facts and tries to make one's life easier. How do you take a young jolly happy little kid, with no cares in the world in a very nice family and put him in a chaotic mistrustful family and call them the right ones the chosen ones? How, how, have they not learned from their past?

Implications of Separation
As it always will be, it will never work unless one is a complete split person. Perhaps if you like them maybe it might still work out. Nobody knew and nobody really cared because you can't really make any money out of it. We must all lay down and follow our ancestor protector to which we revolt frantically. No more can I find myself in which category I am supposed to be. I'm the inventor on the story that fooled my truth, realizing that I should have this or that.

Melbourne

Home life
My memories of living with my mother are very dark. I have blotted many things out of my mind sitting here in the space of a small room writing about a moment in my life that could have easily avoided. There was a lack of society interest in me. They weren't really involved enough, those great people with their aim of sitting down and listening as you talk. It was out of charity more than anything.

Maverick: A memoir of Jacques Kornbrot, 1938 - 2014

Life was the ugliness of my days, the talking with my mother that became to the crying and yelling. Then I was old enough to hit back physically, almost I knocked her down as she was going to stop me from going outside. My lunch was there, so she said let him go, give him his clothes, and let him go. I walked out two days later.

Then we moved into a boarding house and my mother owned it or ran it. It was like a prison, everybody had locks on their doors. I felt like I was in a prison. We had people from many places staying there: Russian, French, Australian and a Lebanon family. Then my cousin arrived from France and stayed with us for a while. Then he got himself settled in and opened a belt factory. He got married to an Australian girl and I rarely saw him.

Jacques in the 1950s

CHAPTER 6: JACQUES' WRITINGS: AUSTRALIA, 1948-1958

In the 20-room house where we lived there were maybe 4-5 books one of them was an English – French dictionary. It was not great help to me for my limitation of French and brain power was very strong indeed. As I understood it learning all the time didn't bring much joy – I felt very strange at the time, pushed into an area that didn't interest me – of being so low etc.

Coming home after school wasn't a joy. My mother was ninety five percent of the time sad. She used to put the food on the table and then go to bed. I wasn't allowed stories or anything and still had to sleep in the same bed. it was a nuisance. When I used to return home after school to a cold, a very cold house that I can remember, I felt so bad that even the food I ate tasted bad. There were no books, no one to talk to at all. It would not have been so bad if I was a simpleton and idiot then maybe I would have appreciated it more

Yet I did fill up these 24 hours during my horrifying experience with her. Yet it wasn't I shouldn't write horrifying because I wasn't scared of her, the way one is of one's parent. There were times I felt that passive family of mine was on my side, but they couldn't be bothered with what was going on. My uncle tried to make me a good Jew by taking me with him to the Synagogue and even gave me pocket money from time to time but It didn't help. I need more than money could buy. The mere fact that my little mind was just in a confusion, we have so many religions saying we are the right one, and the other we not enemy to which is quite a contradiction.

Anyway, let's not move away from my life story, where was I in the 1950's I think, doing my best to get attention to myself for better understanding. Of course, it came to a failure with everyone caring above me, around me. Still, I stayed sane as ever. Nobody but nobody could straighten out the mess they got themselves into once being involved with me. As I understood it, joy happiness lasted one minute, hell lasted forever with my mother.

67

Maverick: A memoir of Jacques Kornbrot, 1938 - 2014

Mother's situation and history

That woman of egoistic emotion the fear of losing a bit of her pride and time over what she has created couldn't follow up her parent life. I would understand if she had no knowledge of family life, but she came from a family of 12 or more. Yet as a parent, all that knowledge of the family structure was of how to deal with it was more to her favour – for she knew nothing at all. I suppose now she probably looks back saying to herself what a good mother she was no doubt. But if I must judge her, I could not put any good word for her favour at all. Boy, do I have **a** memory left over from that egoistic lady. Memory disaster in her ways of life. The obsession that she had she never really went straight to the problem, but it look**ed** like it was the end of the world for her.

My rejection toward my mother came at an early stage as a result of the change from my being with my foster parents. The affection and love they had didn't exist in my mother. I was for her a piece of or part of machinery to repay at an early start in life, like I owed her everything. I didn't understand this, repaying what? For her fault and failure, a woman that used my being as a weapon toward everybody she met and by God it worked. That**'s** where we did not make a match.

I had no pity for her then I still don't have any pity for her now though many in the trade of head shrinking would say "she**'s** not normal" well they're wrong. One tries to better one's life, and if by chance you don't make it, you change your technique. Good Heaven and the rest – that criminal] mind of my mother made me feel guilty for many years with the aid of the rest of that beautiful family. I was forced to behave under all those pressures that were put to me, yet I didn't bend or even think of changing my road to life. It would have been easy to send me back to my foster parents they would have achieved more with me than my real mother. I cannot forgive anybody that had anything to do with my childhood and supposedly education, no one had time for getting involved.

CHAPTER 6: JACQUES' WRITINGS: AUSTRALIA, 1948-1958

Yes, she was forced upon me. I doubt I would have missed her or my father. People were out of the facts with the sad stories that didn't even make me feel sad about them.

- Yes, I was alone, and I became a one man show. Until this day my only insurance is myself.

Even after 40 years he did not totally trust me What more could I have done?

History from Europe to Australia

Yes, Mary Rochman the witty crafty lady from Warsaw that came to Paris to conquer. it was just good for coffee talk no more. She didn't realise that bringing another human being into the world could be such a sacrifice. I had no chance with her. Her one thought, and the fact she couldn't accept the fact she failed as a mother, wanting so much to be free of me. She just didn't understand you can't fly and be on a boat at the same time.

Paths, moving fast as ever for another stream, or road changing when you feel like it? Yes, it's easy when you have programmed everybody to do this coping. Its apparent that she couldn't cope with this unbalancing the scales of her involvement. It must have been annoying her very much, especially arriving in Australia thinking that she would be received with open hand, red carpet which is a dream to think that they would have gone out of their way to do this. Yes, those days of sunshine, rain, canvassing for a better life. Didn't work out this way at all. It was probably because she realised, she never wanted children or knew the meaning of being a mother.

She came from a very problematic area of Poland, where Poland history as it goes isn't a happy one by no means. It has been conquered as we well know by both sides, mainly the West and East. For the last 1000 years Poland hasn't known whether she was going or coming and from her generation there are still many that get lost in their way of moral thinking. Even today where living there is given the scope of living in the free world would make us look upon them as a weird kind of people. The secrecy, not to talk about the smaller of small talk. It's still hard for me to accept the fact that there are people like that, if we do not contradict ourselves, it is small, but with her the change of thought and pain she must have pas**sed** on must have been gigantic. In later year**s** of travel meeting the family not one had a good word for her – always the same line, you must look after her, after all she is your mother, what a line.

A high number of the East Europeans were put under many strains before coming out from Poland, Russia etc. and brought with them the evil and good from those places but mostly the evil. For example, like in the present of the rich and poor. There is more poor people will do if they have more problems than the rich coping with their life.

Family
What I can't understand really **is** the fact that she comes from a very, very large family, loads of sisters and brothers, the facing of **a** good family to what had come. As the Americans would say where, did they go wrong bringing up that daughter of theirs? Since I'm not spending most of my life analysing why or when I can only take a shot in the dark by just saying that she made her ruined road to life and couldn't follow it as many of us cannot, by no mean keep or ideological way.

The Rockman family were living like their forebears. Like all people of this world, the only time they come to their help is when they can splash it on the front page. Rockman, Rockman man, they were rich and still are rich, but useless. When one looks at our family tree, from my mother's side of the five brother their downfall started when they became well to do, meaning that they did not spread the loot about. Oh, they turned up when needed, but not the way one should. For example, Aunt Rose (might make her famous yet) a poor soul that went and lived in Israel. She thought that she was an idealist - more than me that is for sure. She lived on pennies, you would have thought that they would have helped her more, especially my phony mother respect honour and all that shit.

> *Jacques recounted that at celebrations she used to wolf down the food, as her daily food was so frugal. It reinforced his belief that only personal charity was any use.*

Man, woman I don't have anything whatsoever. From 1946 I was living a life of hell. When you mention the family structure what they gave me, and how I was supposed to turn like a complete idiot. What have I got is hate and bitterness of it all. I'm supposed to still smile. and forgive these people who stole my childhood and have taken away. Well, everybody is wrong.

Mother's dreams

My mother stopped to fulfil her dream of life when I was born. She remained idle fearing the world and not crossing the road when she was supposed **to**. Rather she leapt out when she had a chance of getting knocked down while leaping across. If she would have crossed the road while looking both ways, she would have been safer.

> *This may be metaphoric, or he may have heard stories about her actions as she descended into depressive schizophrenia. No one ever used that diagnosis to Jacques, and I only learned of it after his death.*

Most of us do push across dangerous crossings yet still many come out on the other side in **one** piece and a little bit wiser of ourse**lves** but for my mother she didn't have this change luck of the day, she just lived on her pity begging for help she never received for there was nobody that could have helped her the way she wanted, only the way charity is given, doesn't work that way. Seeing her sitting there with that blank look of a statue could make anybody pity her. I doubt Australia or any other place on earth would have made any difference for she was a mental wreck. Yet she couldn't have been different, given the ways of her life she had?

> *There is some sympathy for his mother even though her situation it has such dire consequences for him.*

Mother's mental illness.
Everybody thought she was crazy, but no one moved to help her mentally. Financially they helped. It**'s** easier to give money away, than spending your time sorting the problem. That wasn't a virtue in the Jewish religion, although it was still accepted that she was a nut. Since my mother was never well it went from bad to the worst, I never agreed on anything she said. I violated her privacy so much that she didn't have the right method. In my view, in her disturb**ed** mind, she wanted what was the easiest for herself. It is hard for anybody to say anything bad about one's mother, but what I have written down is what I felt, nothing more. To many she might been a nice person of rare quality, but to me she was hell from the first minute I laid my eyes on her.

> *Jacques knew nothing of her time in a mental asylum. Diana only learned the story 8 months after he died. He assumed that she had been alone in Paris, maybe looked after by her brother or cousins. He just knew she was too mentally sick to care for him, and that his father was deported and murdered.*

Yet there were many men that wanted to marry her, but she turned them down, always saying "because of you I can't marry". I'm positive that she didn't because she was afraid to have more children.

Mother and family interaction
Those famous line of my mother, 'I want to give and so much, but I don't know how'. I was going to do this, but he did those things etc.'. In short, she did not do anything for me that I would lay my life on the line. What is so good at the end of the day? She gave nothing but broke every law in the book of books. The only one she didn't break was to kill me. I'm still here to tell the story an honest story.

They all sided with her even that they knew she was totally wrong, along as the made it look like it was all my fault. I was convinced that I was not just bad, but evil and really bloody bad.

But as history shows, few parents are parents. They are the ones that create the evil around us. When I look about and meet those people that have never suffered or went without starving, had everything laid on, had everything education, loving parent and still come out shits. In the end it makes you wonder. They can't even say but I got an education of some sort so I will be able to go out into the world and do something.

Melbourne Education

The Australian system for my Australian education was destroyed before it ever started and I can't turn to anybody to prosecute or explain the wrong that was done to me, just like that. Yet I'm supposed to understand to forgive etc. Well, I can't as long as I live this criminal cloud will hang over in my mind, no one will be able to tell me different, the laziness of our society.

What I needed at the time was a tutor to bring up to the English standard of course I couldn't accept the fact that here for a time.

Primary School
I was soon put to school – and then everything was different, the total of everything. Here was the thing that happened in what I was later to call the burden of my childhood. It wasn't enough that I had two unperfected languages. I was supposed to have learned another one that had very hard sounds (Hebrew). At the school they would hit the children something I never saw in France. I tried to be one of the boys, but I didn't come through. I never did make any friends, although there was another French kid, but he was much older than me.

The social structure was different. I used to come to home to a very cold house, no love, nor the help that I needed. One of my relatives got me this large dictionary French – English that I never used. It was the only book I had, and I didn't use it. Books at that time never interested me at all.

Meanwhile my mother became more violent toward me, I wasn't bringing good marks, and my English Australian was worse than they thought. I would get reports 'he could have done better'.

Classic teacher admission of failure. Who could have 'done better'?

School was very different than in France. The teacher had **a** seal: Excellent – Good – Fair. And at the end of the week, she would add them up showing who was the best in class. I don't have to mention where I stood in this class. Instead of going forward in the school I was going backwards. I lost interest. It didn't make any sense for me to learn. I was no good to anybody that **is** what I was made to feel.

I would start off in the morning toward school, with my bag full of books and lunch that was more bread than what you can call a sandwich. On the way I got lost and wandered toward to the city and go to the pictures and stay there seeing the picture two or three times then went home. We never got caught sneaking in. When we were really broke, we would go to this big department stores, with all the foods you really could get quite a meal. It **is** amazing how the structure of man's understanding of children doesn't go further than a few words or trying very hard to bring about the way many things might have happened if things would be done the 'proper' way.

Desperate need of support
Nobody thought to get me a private teacher or try to understand the situation I was in. About the only sense my mother ever made was to say you need a private teacher, further than that – a line of hope that was about all. Nobody did it anyway. It never occurred to them that I didn't want to be in my mother's presence at no time. She never meant anything to me she was just a human being that was forced upon me.

Mother knew he needed tutor. BUT she did not ask relatives, although she asked for many other things, especially for herself, and was always needy.

Help from uncle but blame from mother.
It was always my fault for her misfortune, the things that she could not cope with her own personal problems even with the family she used to get herself into arguments with her brother and he'd tell her in his native Polish what he thought dashing out like a mad man. My uncle was the ardent perpetual bachelor. When everything was right between my mother and him, he would take me out and we would see most of the city finishing off at a Kosher restaurant. The way he ate was something out of a Danny Kaye picture. He would order chopped liver, saving the main course which of course was chicken – and then eat everything at the same time. It fascinated me. Here I was learning how to eat the way one really liked to eat – at your own free will. The only things I liked was the sandwiches that were cut really thin. I was given my time good in order. My uncle the lonely bachelor sang of the song he loved. He even showed me its tall top hat suit he looked like a merchant banker. After a night at dinner the way to finish was in some exotic night, but alas that wasn't what today we call a swinger but for him it was the feast after dinner.

We went to the Luna Park in St Kilda the façade was a gigantic face of a clown with his mouth opened, this was the entrance, all the amusement one could imagine the iron chain all about the place. If you didn't know about them, then you were in for a fright or from life, the back of these chains was a sign saying have a laugh and put a penny in and the chain would start make these fluting noises, making the person shocked out of his or her clothes. it was fun there. Then we stroll out toward the back and back to the house of all the locked doors.

My returning to this house was never an enjoyable one, as you may have noticed the coldness of the place could get to anybody' system without a word. I must admit that I wasn't a nervous little boy – I surely held my ground tonight. I was really put on the other side of the fence for the second time in less than a year or two. It must have been confusing drunk with the why, this and that but no one cares really. All they wanted was their peace of mind. I wasn't enough important. They cared more to keep the peace and their nose on clean paper. With the right understanding individual something might have been done.

Summer holidays
Well Susie Rockman took me home and we were invited to stay in their summer house in Frankston with her three sons and one daughter. I vaguely remember about it, not sure if I mixed well with them or not. Susie's husband Norman was a good man. He never talked to me about my mother. In my eyes he was kind to me. They had a barbecue, a big round table with lager, meat and everyone would take a sausage or hamburger and grill it on an open fire, – or go to a picnic.

Norman would take us on his yacht fishing. I was so interested in the life jacket on board when you pulled a cord it would blow up – I never saw one blown, so when nobody was on board pulled at one of the cords and it blew up. Something I didn't realise at the time was how you let the air out.

Bam, I thought I will be in for it when he finds out. It wasn't till a couple of days till we went out fishing we all had our line over the side, he gave a yell – saying who is the idiot that did that, he was not happy. I kept silent as well as the rest of **h**is son**s** – but we did have a good catch, what a waste not to eat it.

Jewish religion
In less than a couple of years I already found myself among a conflict between two religions in the Jewish community one the Orthodox. One was following the rules. The other one my mother playing on the side. In my little way it should not be that way. You were more good if you didn't mind and spend as much time thinking about it.

Hard to decipher. Is he talking about his mother's affairs?

As for the Jewish me, I was forced to go – and spend time in play in a language that I didn't even understand – and it was suffering to be the last one. Yet they gave me the impression till this day that they were afraid and hid behind their beards to go with their funny clothes, waiting beside me going for the Synagogue. On Sunday I would also go to study. It wasn't enough I didn't like the English language at the time, I was supposed to learn this one too, yes how God created the world in eight day**s** in heaven, and I couldn't LEARN two languages in my lifetime.

The teacher use**d** to hit us hard – two different set**s** of school**s** and two set**s of** corporal punishment. I told my aunt about the Hebrew teacher that used to hit us. She said you hit him back, so, when Sunday came I went and I don't remember really whether he hit me or someone else but I got up and he was no bigger than I was and ran up to him and hit him right in the jaw – and a sound came like I broke his false teeth, then I leapt out of the window and that was the last time I was ever seen for Sunday school again.

Jacques & Aunt Rose 1949?

Maverick: A memoir of Jacques Kornbrot, 1938 - 2014

> *Good advice from Aunt Rose, a spirited idealistic lady! Wish I had known her.*

Oh yes, the time I spend one week in Burwood with the smell of unwashed kids studying to be a religious boy getting up at the break of the day to pray, to whom, to what, pray. What I didn't do to get away it was a riot. The house was out in the country a spooky house, inside dark, I imagine there were not on the electricity, anyway I still felt lonely and very depressed. Then one early morning I took off and ran away

I didn't suffer because after being hit by her broom and getting spat at I would run away, and the police would bring me back. All and all, then I ran away for the day, so my photo was in the newspaper. I would survive by going to the market and helping move heavy boxes of fruit and that is how I used to get my food in the daytime. I would go and stay in the movies when I got caught again, I would be taken home.

On one of my escapes from that cold boarding house I went into town, and I met a very nice soldier, and he took me with him to the YWCA and had a big Indian curry meal and there he met his girlfriend. I passed off as his kid brother. Then we went to the movies where he cuddled her, as all the wonderful young people do. On returning with them to the YWCA we had a bite, and they both left, and he gave me some money and said goodbye. I didn't walk more than a bit, a police car pulled alongside – ouch – back to the boarding house. The usual broomstick then straight to the big bed clank the door locked.

> *He always made friends, as he was basically a very friendly kid.*

Mother wants to change back to maiden name.
As I was still full of spirit, I started to search the room to keep myself occupied. I found under the cupboard a wallet with a letter saying that I Mary Kornbrot would like to change my name to my maiden name of Rockman.

CHAPTER 6: JACQUES' WRITINGS: AUSTRALIA, 1948-1958

The rejection must have been horrendous. In the end she did indeed change her name back to Rockman, but not sure when or why.

Without thinking twice – I opened the window and took off again. Running as fast as my legs took me. That night I slept in the back of a car and the early of morning I went to the fruit market. I felt odd and my mind was running through thousands of things what was happening. Was I supposed to be taken to another family, another country? Crazy world to be in. I must have thought for a long time it was already night and I had not made **a** plan where I was going to stay.

As I walk**ed** down Collins Street, I saw a policeman coming toward me, damn, they're after me again. As I rush up to a coffee shop. I noticed that the window was a foot off the ground, and one could slip underneath as I made **a** quick disappearing act and laid there for the remainder of the night without being spotted. I got out from the hiding place and cross**ed** the road and went through a building that had **a** fire door that took you into the other building and let you out at Little Bourke Street. There waiting for me was a woman police officer. What luck back to the boarding house.

Collins street

Maverick: A memoir of Jacques Kornbrot, 1938 - 2014

There was a fuss this time but different. My mother cried and kept saying "I don't understand he has a clean house he has all he needs" except love I wanted to say, someone to tell me stories and busy turning my mind to better use than sorrow, depression she used to get into. I just didn't have any feeling for her.

He 'wanted to say' but did not. He obviously thought it would be futile.

If I had a family of my own, it would have been different. I admit I would have been wild, but I would have had a childhood, not the nightmare that I went through.

Psychiatry and Head Doctors

Lost in my world I was taken to see head doctors (for the first time) They were to sound out my mind to understand my personal problems. Or they were told the wrong stories about me, just that I was misplaced for seven years and given back to my rightful parent. It never came to them, the pretty simple claim that I didn't care about my mother or anybody that was involved with her.

Going back, the head doctor looked at me. Then gave me a board to paint on and took off into the next room with my mother. She probably gave her side of the stories. I doubt very much that there was anything they could really do but just talk. They couldn't do much more than that. Even if the head doctor understood what was going on, there wasn't much she could do but just listen. I'm quite positive that everybody at the time knew what was happening, yet no one, but no one, wanted to act. They were inactive for the sake of not disturbing the evil that was going on. Pleasure of seeing other**s** suffer is common and society is great to turn its face away when someone is asked to give, but when the offer is to take, boy do they come running.

CHAPTER 6: JACQUES' WRITINGS: AUSTRALIA, 1948-1958

So, another day I was taken to more psychiatrists two, three, four, five of them. They also didn't get involved. The head of the Rockman clan (Norman) took me to one psychiatrist and as I sat there in his office. Next to his desk was a tape recorder. I stared at it, and he said it wasn't working. I didn't even know what it was. Instead of showing me how it worked he took it away. He came back saying, 'why do you run from home '– bang the same question. I didn't answer. They thought that what my mother said was right - but the wrong way.

No doubt the best psychiatrists money could buy, but clueless and/or indifferent. How much have things changed? What would be chances of getting some competent help even today?

Then Susie Rockman (wife of Norman, mother of future Lord Mayor of Melbourne) came and took me for lunch. While we were eating, she said that she had to take care of her children too. It wasn't her duty to take care of me, as though I cared about it or anything she said down deep inside. It didn't take a doctor or a psychiatrist to understand what my problems were at all. I just couldn't live with my mother and that's all. I couldn't care less whether my mother lived or died to me it just didn't matter. I belonged to my little world hoping one day I would return to the farm. Then Susie went on saying that there was one of the family that died in prison everybody always had that fear, and it didn't work.

Blame the victim and predict and/or threaten a dire future.

I do not remember which number of quack he was, but he they were all useless. It's not very hard to understand that children run away from home because they're not being taken care of. It's not the child but the parent that is the guilty party. Around me at the time there was no one I could say could be a parent or an uncle or godfather. Everybody was just passing the buck about. As long there nobody is getting killed about it, society accepts this as quite normal. Sometimes I feel that I only bring out the worst in people instead of the good.

I was **in** no doubt if someone would have had the patience towards me and would have sat down and talked and listened it would have been a bit different now. Unfortunately, that wasn't the case. I'm positive that everyone knew what was supposed to be done but nobody did anything about it all. All they did was to pity my mother for having a little brat who would not obey her. From first revolt it didn't matter whether she was right or wrong I just didn't listen or want to understand under any circumstances at all.

Implications about help from head doctors?
The head doctor can only help you if you talk to him. This is very important. Communication is need**ed**, and then you end up damaging the solution, but I could not say anything to about why I acted that way. Yes, I was the bad child to them. I had to know that my mother had a traumatic experience while giving birth, by rejecting me, and that she later became a victim of the second world war losing her trust and with no knowledge of family life at all. She had a lot of good ideas like the many of us – but didn't follow them.

My point is that whether there was a war on not my mother was unfamiliar with being a good parent. She just couldn't accept me and actually being a mother. In a way, the war brought her back to her senses. As I was told, when I was born, she refused to open her eyes, but was able to answer back anything anyone said to her. What an illness, rare of its kind? I must admit pure selfishness from her. After that it was her way or else. She was lost in herself with the guilt of failure I don't think that she ever gave anything for anything.

> *Obviously, Jacques no idea she had been sectioned and no one told him.*

Doing their best?
Till this day I'm as bemused about the way they did their best for me, in their own eyes to start me up so I wouldn't really dirty their good name.

CHAPTER 6: JACQUES' WRITINGS: AUSTRALIA, 1948-1958

Spoiling their genetic force, those idiots as though they didn't understand what was happening or they could have done something, but they didn't despite all the money they had and their great connections. Yet they didn't have **a** goal to find or do the correct thing like give me a private tutor or a teacher that I could look up to, all I got really **was** advice, warning plus threat that didn't do one bit of good to anyone.

Detention Centre after another runaway

I was picked up by the police and was taken straight to the police station, then driven off to a detention centre. It must have been very late at night I was put in a room that had just a bed with clean sheet**s** and I was told to give them my shoes and the door was locked on me again, I sat there on the bed thinking all they can do is locking door on my lock, lock. I hated being locked in. They just didn't understand that I must have sat there for an hour, there was a clock and the door opened and a man said without looking at me whether I was alive, or dead put your shoes on and go and wash your face it was 5.30am.

I must have meditated most of the night about being locked up. Why it must have crossed my mind my freedom was in danger. After having clean**ed** myself, I was led to a great mass hall where other children of all ages sat at the table eating their prisoner meal. Children from broken homes, children of parents that didn't have time or couldn't be bother**ed** with them and were put out into the street. These little mind**s** confused with their parent**s**, these contradiction**s** that didn't make sense to them from their demanding parent**s**. I sat down to eat, and the conversation wasn't big talk, but children like me asking why were the treated this way, or better how happy they were here not being hit and having a meal more than they had at home. I could believe or accept that if children are brought up properly that they would **not** go that far as to run away from home or turn their mind toward what our beautiful, civilized world calls crime at that age. It's my doubt that not too many parent**s** achieve goal

83

of success of mastering the parenthood. For the next few days, it was the same thing straight from my little cell to the mass Hall, and then back.

> *The horror of being locked up and not knowing for how long must have been terrible.*

I was taken then to near Flinders Station, and there was Norman and six very serious men sitting behind a desk. They looked at me and then a gentleman took me to a room and started to ask the same questions of course as usual I could not answer I just stared at him. I was going through the same grown-up question time with the "why" etc. It never came into these complicated people that what I need the most was a parent figure, not a broken-down woman that didn't and couldn't cope with me. I was taken back to the room of six serious men then, they spoke about my running away.

Norman said that they had arranged for me to be sent to a boarding school in Ballarat. Well, what an achievement I wasn't going back to that stupid woman. I was chauffer driven down to Ballarat.

Ballarat

On arriving there I was taken to the school and was greeted by the headmaster and showed around like I was supposed to try it. It was something out of an English countryside it looked like a gigantic manor house. It was beautiful. Then we went to the study of the headmaster, and I was told by my chauffer and Susie, I think, that my new house was assigned.

CHAPTER 6: JACQUES' WRITINGS: AUSTRALIA, 1948-1958

Ballarat early days

Education

I was put in 6 Form then slowly to 5 Form, 4 Form, 3 Form and did my maths in the 2 Form. You can well imagine how I felt. There I was in the midst of children from my year and my age. I started by going from bad to worse in my studies. For the hours that were wasted on me money wise could have been given away or even thrown in the fire. It would have done more than it did to me. Also, I was much more advanced in different subjects, but it surely didn't help me much in the third class.

Oh man I know inside when I remember how they destroyed my youth I use to beat anybody while fighting in the class because they were much younger than me. *As I became the protector I was there to help.* I should have been taught better than through that forced education again, like that with all that classy school, probably expensive.

I always felt when I was in that classroom, I knew more than the other boy**s**. I was much older than them mentally. I would always stop the fight, three cheer**s** for that. *I felt more as a Judge than a student.* Till now it**'s** hard for me to understand why I was forced to just sit there in class where I did very little of work, couldn't they understand this as though there wasn't any money around. It was a very expensive school you can believe that. I'm not talking any out of this world story, this **is** how it stood and still does in my mind, the waste.

Maverick: A memoir of Jacques Kornbrot, 1938 - 2014

Peaceful Ballarat and education – or not
Well back at the boarding school life was peaceful, so peaceful that I felt I was getting less educated here although the many hours sitting in class learning nothing whatsoever. I was in third grade and in my maths in second. Yes, I can recall my school days they were limited very indeed at the boarding school. I was put in a class of my own age then I was slowly demoted to a confusion of classes right to the third grade it's funny it's sad and bloody bad in these class**es** I was you can say taller and bigger. I didn't even bother to get myself into fight**s** I used to stop them, and my silly teacher use**d** to tell me what to do. That stupid woman as she sat at the head of the class with sad eyes looking down among her supposed follower**s**, oh she had the nerve at the end of the term write on my paper "he could have done better". That's how far they went, who know**s** what would have happened if someone would have taken me aside and taught me alone up to the standard to which class, I was supposed to be in but it didn't occur to them all those clever wise people, as long **as** I didn't run away in their eyes I was doing fine, interest in me was dead in them.

> *Could do better! Criminal negligence. They knew he was bright but failed him.*

Ballarat routine
The getting up in the morning by the sound of the bell, in turn we would have our showers each morning on a rotating system. It was good to be the last one, one could sleep another 20 minute**s** or so. Then we would have one hour of homework to do then they have breakfast then at time we go to church afterward we go back to the classroom to study. For me the classroom was a place one would sit down while other**s** would study. I would meditate in my little world of it all not knowing what will turn up in the future.

In the morning the bell would start, then in every dormitory one would get up to have his daily shower in turn, it would mean one day one could stay in bed for another 10 – 20 minutes before breakfast. We would spend an hour of homework then go and have breakfast, bacon and eggs, toast! Better the whole works, this I can say the food was great.

They said that if I didn't want to not to go to church, I didn't have to. What a riot. Not again, the same stupid remark, poker bluff whether I should go or not. It was really a chaos when it was religion hour. I was told to leave the room because my Catholic Jewish ideas didn't meet with the protestant ideas. The first few lesson**s** I was there. Then the Rev. started to talk about heaven and hell and that were things didn't meet with my Jewish idea. At 9.00am they all went to church except me. Sometimes I went - then we would have math, for math I went down a class. At religion learning I was told to lose myself. I was rejected or better, degraded.

Was he the ONLY Jewish kid, one wonders?

When I was old enough, I was in the air cadets for two hours a week, Sure, I had food, good clothes, but that wasn't the kind of need I needed. What I really needed was to catch up for all the stuff in Australia that led me astray. I did not need pity, what I needed **was** someone to teach me and love me as they did on the Farm. The warmth of being needed, not a front for useless self-pity. Nobody likes people to pity on.

Leisure

For those few years I was there my only good memory was that I was able to roam the wide-open fields of Ballarat with it**s** creek and wildlife.

Saturday came it was a wet cloudy day we would all stay in but **if** it was sunny, we would go to the gold field in Ballarat and dig for gold. Some of the kids took it seriously and after a year had a stash. Using a torch on the wall, the light would sparkle on tiny specks of shining yellow colour, on checking it would disappear clean off. I never had the patience to do this, so I kept on long walks through the countryside. Ballarat surroundings had loads of animal**s**, magpie**s**, rabbit**s**, bird**s** with nature I can't remember everywhere the greenery, the spaces between were enormous.

Maverick: A memoir of Jacques Kornbrot, 1938 - 2014

When I went into town, I could go to a store and choose anything in the line of wear, sign my name and I got it, so easy. But who needed that! I didn't, it was a waste of money and kindness. The more educated you are, the **more** stupid you are when it come**s** down to solve a simple problem as mine. All those years wasted to summarise all here on a page could be written but would someone in future or now understand the time for the children of misfortune. Still there are but few children that came out with their childhood like a good bag. I can't remember a time that someone in the period of being with mother understood that she never said nice things about me at all.

They turned a tank that used to hold liquid in the 1800s into a tank and a swimming pool. There I learned to swim. By mistake I jump**ed** in the wrong end, going down the bottom coming up and going down I suddenly realise that**'s** it I'm done for. I started yelling help each time I came up, one boy jumped in, the first one that reached me I clung to him like I never clung to anybody in my life, and we both went under like a sunken ship. If it wouldn't have been for the other boy that came along, we probably both would have drowned. They got me loose from him and guided me back to the side. As I hopped out and realised completely in what mess I had got myself into, I started to tremble like mad. I sat down for a minute or so and walked to the end, and then started to walk away getting my confidence back again. I admit that my swimming improved a lot after that.

When I came home for the summer holiday I would go to St Kilda and swim out to sea, believe it or not but the Australian seas is one of the best seas to swim in. On a regular day the waves go to 20 to 30 feet on one of those wrong moments I went out and for an hour I tried to swim back to shore, the current wouldn't let me in, I could see a lifeguard look out sitting there knowing that I couldn't come in he just sat there waiting. Boy was I furious, when I finally got back to shore, he just smil**ed** saying that wasn't bad. Asking him why he didn't come out to rescue me he replied that I didn't wave my hands or yell! It took me a couple of days before I ever did that again.

St Kilda Beach

Joe's Café – an alternative society

So, I took them there, but they didn't believe me. Then my mother said that I probably stole and helped some person into getting into a house. I couldn't believe when they asked me to tell them where. They said I lied.

After a running away episode, where they wanted to know where he had been.

So, the next time my running away was a bit away from where we lived, right in the city. I only stole food stuff. Other items didn't interest me. Unlike this Russian kid, he used to spend two hours at it, and he arrives at Joe's Cafe, and he would put everything from his pocket on the table: table knife, watches, candy, glasses, and even a brand-new boomerang. He was good at it. He used to say the hand is faster than the eye and to prove it I went with him, going through a department store and once we were out of the store, he produced an electric razor.

Jacques always admired skill of any kind.

You can well imagine that I didn't meet normal kids from normal homes, just kids that were deprived of their childhood, and in Melbourne there were quite a few of them, each with their own stories to tell. But we never went into that subject. Most were great little guys, except for this Englishman that walked around with a 16" knife strapped to his shoulder. He was big and always breaking into houses and getting caught. Then the

Maverick: A memoir of Jacques Kornbrot, 1938 - 2014

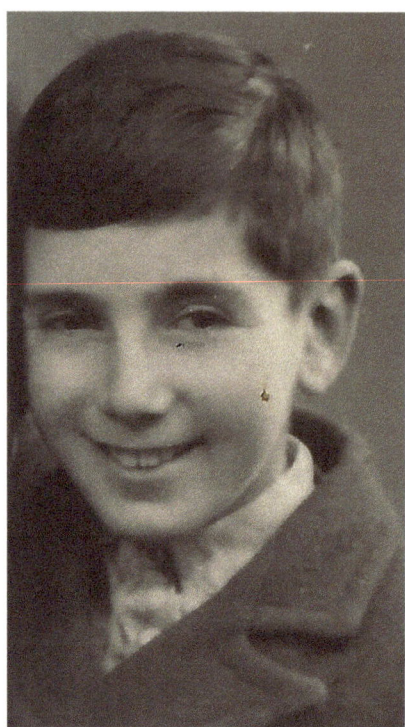

Jacques at age 11 and 15 years old

best of all was the Friday robber. He had a Luger, but we never did ever see any bullet in it. He was a riot. He would go in the botanical gardens on Friday evening and. hold up people coming home from work with their pay and do a stick up. He always got away.

Well one day the Englishman and the Friday robber went and broke into a house and the Friday robber said that he would take all the stuff they took and pawn it and he would meet the Englishman at the station near the Yara. Well at Joe 's cafe where we used to meet usually. He come in and asked if we had seen him. Then he told us that they pulled a Job together and that he took all the goodies pawn. Later we found out that he was seen in Adelaide.

CHAPTER 6: JACQUES' WRITINGS: AUSTRALIA, 1948-1958

The Friday robber was a real character. He said let us go and scare the hell out of the Chinese. So, we go and enter in their tea house in China town, on seeing us walk in, they were dressed in very pointy shoes which they used as a weapon, and jack knifes to go with it. They were slowly coming towards us and the Friday robber ahead of us in a James Cagney walk yelling let's get a Chink pulling out his Luger and waving it at them. You never saw anybody run for their life like they did.

Anyway, back to the Englishman. He finally got caught and we didn't see him for quite a long time. I wonder what ever happened to the Friday robber.

Those uncreative human beings that would sit back and made these programs that could not be followed through laziness. Yes, I would come out of those small unlit offices to face the world again, what next? Well, we would go home on the train and for the next four days I would be put in the house. Then hell would break out and I would start to move closely to the city and found my way back to the café seemingly new faces like the beautiful blonde that was going to get married to a Canadian sailor but couldn't get a visa to go there because she was considered a criminal because she made her way on her back. She was a very nice person.

One of them got to mug someone in the garden and accidentally pushed the man into the Yara and took off without knowing that he couldn't survive and so drowned.

The Friday robber, or someone else? What a story!

Yet they're really there going on in my little world. You really can say it was much more interesting than being at home listening to the moan of a pitiful woman. All the time it was nervous for her, I didn't care anyway.

91

Maverick: A memoir of Jacques Kornbrot, 1938 - 2014

> *He does not write about the Carlton gangs and the tough guy. The stories in chapter 6 come from Willy Halpert, although he did talk about the tough guy in passing.*

Departure

After my disaster with my mother and relatives that did their best to keep the peace, I was packed off to Greece (or Morocco). My stay was brief. I saw! I met! then took off like a dart. As to where I spend most of the time every morning I would get up and wash my mouth out with their brandy, it must have been cheaper than water. Never was I bother**ed** by the Moroccans, I looked like one of them dark hair and my little moustache, a few hairs coming out I was proud of it. I would be very careful while showing not to shave as it grew peacefully. How that cool climate was good, and the Brandy - "a likely story".

> *However, he arrived in Israel from Greece – see chapter 8.*

CHAPTER 7.
YOUTH 1956-1972

Jacques Israel, work, travel

Timeline

1956	-	1958	Kibbutz Kissufim, Eilot
1958			Aunt Rose, Tel Aviv
1958	-	1961	Army National Service
1961	-	1962/63	Negba, 12 months, Tel Aviv
1962/63	-	1963	Europe travels
1964?	-	1966?	More Europe travels, Tel Aviv?
1966?	-	1967	Tel Aviv, Ashdod
1967			Army as conscript veteran
1967	-	1968?	Eilat, Negba again, Tel-Aviv
1968?	-	1971?	Africa, Kenya, Congo: at least 2 stints
1968?	-	1972	Tel Aviv

Arrival in Israel, first kibbutzim

Jacques left Australia in 1956, working his passage on a Japanese boat. There is brief mention of Morocco. He arrived in Israel just before the 1956 war, knowing no Hebrew and having lost his address book. His first night was spent on a park bench in Jaffa. Helpful police found his Aunt Rose in Tel Aviv, where he stayed briefly.

Kibbutz Kissufim

Almost immediately he was sent to a pioneer left-wing (Mapam kibbutz interesting Spielberg created a movie just after Independence Day 1956, before the 1956 war. Members were of mixed origin. Some had come up through the Israeli Nahal youth movement that aimed to improve the life chances of 14-18-year-olds from difficult home situations, and also had serving members of the Israeli Defence Force (IDF), who alternated between farming and active service. Others were immigrants from the USA, possibly avoiding the Korean war, and South America. None of the members seem to have been called up for the 1956 war. Foreigners may not yet have done National Service, and Israelis may have been exempt because they were too young? Jacques remembers bombardment, but no one taking part.

Kissufim (politically on the left, as part of Ahdut HaAvoda) was his first experience of socialist/communist practice. He reacts with amusing accounts of incidents, including weekly Saturday meetings. He notes there were leaders and followers, but little room for diversity of talents. People left the kibbutz because a majority decreed they could not *use* their talents, e.g. an engineer about locating a swimming pool. I was struck with this later in Kibbutz Negba, when a *woman* driving an air-conditioned tractor was a matter of debate. Pioneer women ploughed the land by hand. Contrast this with Jacques' *conservative* French village, where everyone enjoyed communal harvests. The Americans thought themselves superior (they brought this with them from 'home', as Americans do the world over). There was an over-valuation of academic education. Jacques notes that many were *not* idealists; the Israelis because they viewed Nahal as an escape from poverty, and the immigrants because they were escaping bad things at home, notably the Korean War. However, there was at least one highly committed communist.

Jacques did not maintain contact with Kissufim, which later became a tourist resort (like many kibbutzim). Since 7th October 2023, it is rubble.

Kibbutz Eilot
Jacques became bored with Kissufim and managed to get sent to an even more embryonic kibbutz. Eilot was a border post on the Red Sea near the Jordan port of Aqaba. In 1963, it moved inland. They lived off fishing, a commercial laundry, and a welding plant. They also started a now thriving date plantation, of which Jacques was justifiably proud.

The social situation was very different from Kissufim. Members were mostly older, and many had been sent by their home kibbutz only for a specified period of time. Unlike Kissufim, they really were mostly idealists. The members wanted to move even closer to the border and build a pier for their fishing. This brought them into conflict both with the founder of Ahdut HaAvoda, Talbenkin, and the Eilat city council. Members lost in the end, but after Jacques had left. They were forcibly moved inland in 1963. Now, like most kibbutzim, the primary economy is tourism.

Army service

In 1958, Jacques was called-up to the army. Jacques became an officer. This was possibly quite unusual for someone with no formal qualifications. According to Willy Halpert, recruits were closely watched in their first month for leadership and other skills. The army spotted Jacques' natural talents, so he was chosen for Officer School. You might ponder on why the Australian school system (private and public) failed for eight years to spot abilities clear to the Israeli army in one month.

Jacques, Israeli army, IDF

How many other kids' talents got missed? I wonder if Israelis are still so democratic on not bothering about prior education. Apparently, even then a degree was needed for higher officer ranks. He was assigned to the Nahal kibbutz Mashabei Sadeh. Now it is also a tourist resort – of course. This was followed by periods of active service. Jacques was initially a paratrooper. He had a bad jump and was hospitalised, and then did other military duties, including training new recruits. His view of women soldiers was stereotyped by their apparent unwillingness to get uniforms dirty by lying in the mud!

In the Nahal, he met lifelong army friends. Mordi[52] and Freda Zoriah, Amitai Schecter, Amos and Batya Gur, Danny Hai and Ilana[53] Gomo are among the ones I met over the years. Jacques was living with Ilana (probably his first serious relationship) and engaged to be married. They were adopted as surrogate parents by teenager(s) not getting on with their parents. Lots of kids adopted Jacques over the years! Jacques pulled out of the marriage at the last minute. He was not ready in his own mind. Ilana married soon after on the rebound and has children, but the marriage broke up. Jacques retained contact via the group, and they continued as friends. I met, and became friends with, Ilana on visits to Israel; a good woman, who had a tough life. If Jacques had married her, maybe he would have been a father; something I could not do for him. Ilana died in September 2021. There is no account of Jacques' military service in his writings.

After the army

Kibbutz Negba
After the army, Jacques was a worker (not a member) on Kibbutz Negba. He met and was heavily influenced by Kuba Vilan[54] (born 1916), a left-wing thinker who had served in the British army in Egypt in the Second World War and was heavily involved in politics and agriculture unions. Jacques worked in the fields with Eitan Arieli[57], Drori[58] and Ariela Lamdan and Gershon Vilan[55]. I am still friends with all of them, and with Kuba's youngest son, Abu, who has also been a Member of Knesset (the Israeli parliament) for the Peace Now party. Bobby[59] Stock – was a volunteer

CHAPTER 7: YOUTH, 1958-1972: WORK, ISRAEL, EUROPE, UNIVERSITY, USA

Negba living quarters

English teacher on Negba and became a good friend to Jacques, and later a great friend to me. She died of diabetes complications.

After a year, Kuba, as head of the Kibbutz, offered Jacques two alternatives: full membership of Negba, or leave. He did not want the constraints of membership and left for Tel Aviv and the wider world, where he was a footloose bachelor.

Tel Aviv and Europe

Jacques' travels included France, Russia, Germany, where he renewed his friendship with Tom Reinhardt, who he had first met as a volunteer at Negba. He stayed in Munich, worked, and learnt German, without formal training, using his talent for languages. Jacques and Tom then toured Europe, ending up in Greece, where I met them. Memorable for all three of us!

Jacques' '67 War

Jacques was called-up some time in the build-up just before the pre-emptive invasion. He was assigned to the Gaza front, leading a group of 'older' men (he was approaching 28, but many were older, 35-55). Wikipedia gives an account of the Six Day War. Jacques would have been part of the Northern, El Arish, campaign.

Gaza campaign. Map. Combatants, Jordan valley

He had to make tough decisions that haunted him all his life, but he never discussed them with me. Maybe he feared I would not have understood. I know I would have supported him all the way. It is so sad that he could even contemplate that it might be otherwise. His group was supposed to mop up after forward troops had repelled the Egyptians. He received a medal and was cited for bravery. Things did not go to plan, and Jacques got a medal for bravery for extracting his group from difficulties.

Citation for Bravery, 1967

Brigade Dan 54-4/47 Kornbrot Jack
Participated in the campaign of BENE-OR "SONS OF LIGHT"
Was wounded in action during conquest of Gaza
His accomplishments were of highest order
Signed Yehuda Reich, Colonel, Brigade Commander, June 1967

CHAPTER 7: YOUTH, 1958-1972: WORK, ISRAEL, EUROPE, UNIVERSITY, USA

He was quite badly wounded with shrapnel in his back and sides, and hearing loss. He was given morphine on the battlefield and again when he got to hospital. He was in for some weeks.

Jacques after 1967 war in different parts of Israel

Willy and someone else unknown visited him. His then girlfriend, a Moroccan called Andrei, left him. He was left with permanent disability, comprising loss of hearing and intermittent back pain. He recuperated, partly at Kibbutz Negba and partly at Eilat.

Jacques in Africa and beyond

Jacques did consultancy work in agriculture and management in Kenya and Congo. He had several anecdotes and was always going to tell me more later, but it never happened. Daily life was pleasant and took over; so, somehow, we never 'got round to it'. Now it hurts me so much not to have talked about it. Israeli friends have no exact recollections about this time. He did not write about Africa at all! But there were just the anecdotes.

99

Maverick: A memoir of Jacques Kornbrot, 1938 - 2014

Diana growing up, 1958-1972: University and early work

I got a 2.2 B.Sc. in Physics from Bristol University. Mostly enjoyable, but I got somewhat lost and never really got absorbed in studies. Dilys Jenkins (Shackleton) was my physics lab partner. She died in Australia in 2021. To my shame, I did not give attention to her daughter, Jo, my goddaughter. Maybe it was related to my infertility? Jean Whyte was another physicist friend who married an American astronomer had two children and got divorced. I caught up in 2015: she had become eclectically spiritual in ways I found hard to fathom. Fellow physics students were fun. Roller skates on Wednesday, many student parties. Some political activity: War on Want, Ban the Bomb.

London, 1961-1966: social
I became good friends with Carole[92] (studied history) and Valerie[91] (studied German) from Bristol. Many wild 60s parties before and after meeting Jacques. Val and I accidentally gate-crashed the Ambassador's floor of the US embassy and took a gold 'Ambassador's Office' card as souvenir (it adorned the loo in Val's flat). Carole made very valuable edits to this Ms. She died of pancreatic cancer in April 2022 after a brave fight.

London, 1961-1966: work
I had my first real job as a computer programmer with Elliot Automation worked on automating Air Traffic Control. The project replaced handwritten transfer slips with printed ones, hooray. Even current 'intelligent' AI cannot replace, or even much reduce, the workload of human controllers. I could see that progress would be through management, not through technical expertise, and anyway, I still wanted to be a theoretical physicist. So I quit programming and enrolled for a physics M.Sc. at Chelsea College of Science and Technology (Wikipedia has errors; already part of UL when I enrolled in 1963). Teaching work to enable the M.Sc. included Fich Institute of Data Processing (accounting programs for IBM1401 in machine language), physics/maths at Kilburn Polytechnic, St. Saviour's

CHAPTER 7: YOUTH, 1958-1972: WORK, ISRAEL, EUROPE, UNIVERSITY, USA

& St. Olave's grammar school (the only employment place still surviving in the same form as 1961-1966), North London Polytechnic and William Grimshaw Secondary Modern (graduates The Kinks), now Fortismere.

I did not pay for any part of my university education: B.Sc., M.Sc., M.A., Ph.D. Opportunities for people born in 1940 in many ways outstrip those for people born in 2000. More graduates, but less social mobility!

Diana: America

I still wanted to be a great physicist and applied to the USA and was accepted with a Scholarship to Columbia University in New York City. My father died within three months. Three weeks after the funeral, I went back to the USA at my mother's insistence. I did not have companions to study physics with and failed the Ph.D. qualifying exam.

Diana in New York City

So, I transferred to Mathematical Psychology with Gene Galanter[81]. I was good at *that*, and gained a Ph.D. I made lasting friends, especially Ellen Orans (Morgan), now married to Englishman, Wally, and living in London.

Jacques and Diana

Diana and Jacques: beginnings, 1963

In the summer of 1963, I was touring Greece solo. Valerie[91] had failed to turn up. I did some islands and ended up in Athens, visiting the American Express. Meanwhile, Jacques and his friend Tom were also touring Greece and frequenting the American Express. I dropped my glasses. Jacques picked them up, and we all went out to lunch. I was fascinated by both, and we spent my last night sleeping next to them on the Lycabettus Hill.

London

Jacques came to London. We made passionate love in Jacques' room in Camden Town, a wonderful first experience for me (23), one of many for Jacques (25). London was a riot for us: a Sierra Leone wedding with African princes; bands where Jacques knew players. I was still trying to get back into physics research, doing a nuclear physics M.Sc. at Chelsea College, enjoying the 1960s swinging King's Road in the evenings and teaching physics by day. It was real love, but we were not ready.

Diana and Tom

I had a two-year distance separated relation with Tom, Jacques' friend. He visited England and my parents hated him but were tactful. Probably they could see his utter self-absorption. I visited him several times but was not enamoured of his snobbish mother and felt eclipsed by his beautiful fashion model sister-in-law (that marriage did not last). We spent an *apparently* idyllic six weeks in Greece, summer '64 – with much maths talk. The affair ended when Tom, obsessed with his famous family

CHAPTER 7: YOUTH, 1958-1972: WORK, ISRAEL, EUROPE, UNIVERSITY, USA

(grandfather impresario Max Reinhardt), chose father over holiday with me. He was utterly self-absorbed. I cannot now understand what I saw in him.

Jacques and Diana reunited and wed

Reunited

We corresponded from our parting in 1963. When the 1967 War came, I realised just how much I really loved Jacques. I visited Israel in spring 1972 with my grandmother. Passionate love immediately resumed at the hotel. Jacques proposed in romantic Jaffa. I eagerly agreed – idyllic. I went back to the USA to finish my Ph.D., while Jacques went back to Israel and got his 'Jewish papers'. He was willing to come to the USA, which I did not want; I was willing to go to Israel, which he did not want. We agreed to try London, which we both came to love. A new and inspiring chapter was about to begin

CHAPTER 8.
JACQUES' WRITING ISRAEL, 1956-1972

Starting off

Arrival in Israel

With the communist world – it's beautiful, and the damaging effects of it are like the four seasons. After being rejected by my family due to laziness, single-minded as they were, I was manoeuvred to go to the land of milk and honey, a country with more self-problems than the most backward country in the world. A land that has seen more war and destruction than anywhere in the world. This land has been under rule by so many different nations. Until today, they have not solved the problems yet. But that is another song.

As I left the port, seeing the last of the Italian coastline, towards the land that one day it might be run by another nation, whatever is the name of the game. I went off to my cabin and slept for 24 hours. Then I got up and went to the purser to find out that they didn't load my case on board. I had everything in it, plus all my addresses, etc... So, I arrived at Haifa with nothing but what I was dressed in.

At Customs, an old lady that was in front of me said, 'Why do they need police here? Here it is a Jewish land. We are good people.' I wanted to laugh, but I just looked straight on. Leaving the port, I headed to Tel Aviv. All these good people: in less than one hour, I saw drunks, a man cursing the country and whatnot.

Tel Aviv – as you come in, it looked like matchboxes, the style which one does see anywhere except the States and a modern city. I went straight to the Ministry of Information, only to find out that they had moved, and they would be open the next day at the new address.

Reminds me of the 2022 UK shambles bureaucracy – Ukraine, NHS

So, I start to walk about, looking at this little city, hearing so many tongues spoken loud, sounding like they were in argument. But it's a natural thing there; it's not a nation that you find that will whisper to you. They like to be heard no matter. Even today it has not changed much. Since it was still summer, I did not need to find cover, so I headed west with the sun towards Jaffa, which at the time was the red area, of course. Not to forget it was a port, a very old port, mainly lived in by Arabs and Jews.

The Jaffa tower where Jacques spent his first night in Israel

After finally walking my feet off, I found myself a spot in the park looking over the sea and settled myself down. It must have been 2.30 in the morning, and this car pulled up and someone yelled out to me. It was the police. It's the only country in the world that the police tell you to come to them, instead of strolling over to ask what you're doing. I told them what happened, that my suitcase was not put on the boat, that the Ministry of Information had moved office that day. So, they said, why was I there in the park? I told them I could not stay in a hotel because I did not have enough money. They took me with them to the police station and I was given tea and my first pitta with honey.

Jacques had many happy welcomes at police stations around the world, starting in Paris at age seven.

Give or take a few, I suddenly realized that they did not understand any of my Australian. So, they fetched an Englishman that did not know more than those with the broken English. So, I wrote down exactly what happened, and they all laughed. It was amazing; my accent must have really been bad. At 8 am sharp, this old policeman came in and spoke in Hebrew that I didn't understand. He did not know anything but Hebrew. Sat behind the desk was a sergeant with lots of paper – and paper all over the place. I wanted to find my aunt, this quick. I described her and they produced a list of 20 Rose Woolfs in Tel Aviv. The policeman took me from one side of Tel Aviv to the other.

Finding Jacques' aunt, Rose Woolf, in Tel Aviv
You want to believe she was the last one on the list? He knocked on the door, she came out and spoke with him. Then said she did not know me. She was nearly convinced, except that there was a picture of the family on the sideboard. Then she had a look at me, still not believing who I was, and said in broken English, 'You were supposed to be here two months ago.'

Maverick: A memoir of Jacques Kornbrot, 1938 - 2014

Jacques with Aunt Rose in Tel Aviv

CHAPTER 8: JACQUES' WRITINGS: ISRAEL, 1956-1972

She had a really great sense of humour, but that's for later. I said goodbye to the nice policeman, and all we did was just smile at each other and point the way.

Apparently, Aunt was not long in Australia after the incident where she advised Jacques to hit the Hebrew teacher back. Language a problem!

Like most everybody that goes to Israel, or gets there, one does not have money in one's pocket. If it had been England, I would probably never have got in.

Quite so, seen from disgraceful Tory anti-refugee, anti-immigrant policy in 2022. I am now so ashamed of the UK.

So, now I had finally found my aunt, with broken English, Yiddish, rubbish Polish, and waving our hands about. I went straight to bed. Boy, did I sleep for nearly a week. She woke me up with a cup of tea, shaking me like a bag of bananas. I got up and went out of Tel Aviv. It was quite warm where she lived. The silence and beauty of the place, with lots of old ladies like my aunt. I got a kick when she would tell them who I was, and where I came from, etc. She felt proud to be seen with younger people.

The Jewish Agency bureaucracy

Then I went to the famous Jewish Agency to see if I could get in to an Ulpan on a kibbutz to learn Hebrew; plus, you work half a day, then you come out knowing the language of the men and women, which is separate. One thing you must be ready to do is to go from one office to another if you want to get something done. It's like getting punished for something you have not done. After several office rooms, I sat in front of this man that was supposed to find me a place for an Ulpan [intensive Hebrew language training while working, probably on a kibbutz]. But it seemed that this man was not taken by my looks. My interpreter said later, 'He did not like you because your hair was long.' One thing I learned that if you are not wanted around, don't stick around.

Maverick: A memoir of Jacques Kornbrot, 1938 - 2014

Kibbutz Kissufim

Kissufim, first impressions

So, I found my way to a kibbutz near the city of Gaza, where dear Samson ran off with the door of that city. Some say that was to forge swords and not pans. Kibbutz Kissufim, but everyone called it 'kiss of fire'. As always, I was the eldest or the youngest. There is no university in the world like a kibbutz, where you can learn better about politics, and communism, or something like it. What behaviour. The kibbutz had at the time about 150 people: a mix of Israelis, American North and South, Poles, two Australians and one Englishman, but no Irish.

My first day there I found that no one understood the English I spoke, and the only Aussie there was not there that day. So, one American, a Canadian, and a Pom (Australian for Englishman) were trying very hard to find out what the hell I was talking about. After a while, everybody was happy that they and I had understood where I was going to work next day. I was to plant potatoes sitting on a machine; it would then drop through a pipe that led the potatoes into the soil, bedded into the ground, followed by two discs which covered the potatoes. The next couple of days was great; potatoes in and out. Then, when it was all planted, I went back to the Ministry of Works to find out what was my next mission.

Kibbutz society

Yes, in this mini-nation were American – children, Argentinians, a couple of Syrians, a very few others, one Englishman, two Australians and me. You could well imagine the problems that came forth about who should lead. Ninety percent were well educated, their knowledge more verbal than producing wealth at the time. Some were very left wing in their beliefs, and that produced a conflict.

Would you believe that only a few miles away was the Gaza Strip full of people ready to kill everybody there? Only two and a half miles away

CHAPTER 8: JACQUES' WRITINGS: ISRAEL, 1956-1972

from the border, but that's another story. I shall write more about our neighbours later.

Kibbutz as a mini village

The kibbutz is a mini village; your private life is owned by the kibbutz. Yet with all this, there is plenty to do during the day, like work, but in the evenings, it became quite boring. There is just so much you can read or, in fact, sing and laugh. But if you want, say, to go for a long walk in a city or play or even go down to the bar and get yourself plastered so that you don't know who you are, then your luck is out, because it is miles away. None of the members made any impression on me; with all their talking, they were not inventing what was, in my eyes, a secure future. What was, in fact, happening was that the place was being weeded out of those that would rule the kibbutz with good ideas. Many good people with the right kibbutz ideas left because they could not put across their paths and ideas.

Jacques did not stay in contact with any of them.

Social organisation

The interesting thing was the way this kibbutz was laid out – first of all there were so many leaders, with the idea that their ideas were the best. There was a group that was very strong in this idea, more communist than the communists themselves. Each side knew himself very well. Frightening, I must admit. I found it quite amazing that none of these people who lived under communist rule wanted to create a life where it didn't matter what political structure operated. Out of 10 people, there is only one who takes the lead, and everybody listens. The responsibility was not great, but they surely fought for it.

Later, Jacques comments they were mostly not idealists.

When you get too many educated human beings in a small place, it's for sure you will have problems. People want things, but how is it going to be worked out? Not too many of us has the power of speech to put over our case so everybody can understand this situation of how to run the show. In a group, everything becomes political; such is the way of life. Giving new hope of the golden rainbow in the end, which isn't, as it won't help any. If you sit down and read all the best ways how to win, in the end there will be no solution. However attractive it may sound, we all play in that wheel somehow.

There was a lot of friction between the different groups. The Americans showing off that they were more educated, and so more understanding, which they were not. That is something that keeps surprising me. All the time these people that think they know so much or have been trained and educated think they can do a better job. The fact is, it is not true. Like the majority of all people, whatever they do, we are a lot of talkers. Talk more than in actual practice. With all their knowing how, it was poor kibbutz but was rich in talkers.

Adapting to Kisssufim and its Mapam socialism
Anyway, for me it was the start of learning what you can really do or not do under these conditions. Sometimes, I would arrive from the field bored, seeing the same faces looking into space, which we called the kibbutz stare, even that we had village idiots that people would stare at. Some of them did you a favour if they talked to you or said hello. They even had a meeting about it; the Israeli group complained why nobody said hello, but you have that everywhere.

Back on the kibbutz, you have a chairman and a vice-chairman. They are the managers of the kibbutz, which has a powerful structure. The chairman runs the whole place about money: where he can invest, spend, etc. Then you have the minister of employment, who has more of a job lot than anything else. What that poor man had to put up with is *indescribable*: some that refuse to work with others, etc.

One must be there on a kibbutz to really see it work, like who is the man or woman that plans where people should go and work? Where it is most important, he has the most impossible job because he has to find places for people that don't want to do this work, or they don't want to work with the other guy, or the person is not healthy enough to do hard work, so a light job must be found for him. Yes, when he ends his days, he must feel like a doctor consulting many patients.

Saturday night decision: meetings and democracy?
Every Saturday night is the night of the week that a meeting of the whole kibbutz gathers. Someone gives the money problem facing the place or how much money we had made and what can't we do with it. Other items – like why should this person be sent on a course? – were discussed. Some of these people spend most of their life at courses, like they don't have their mind to advance any planning for anything for themselves, except to sit and listen.

Maybe it is a human disease not being able to use one's brain. Out of 10 people, whatever situation they are, in there will always be a leader that will have the last word; like in the animal kingdom that we laugh so much about, you will find this. Many of those Americans that were there at the time were people that ran away from the Korean War and spent their time making excuses about why they came. The others fitted there because it was an easy life to be in no problem of the tax or knowing where your next meal will come from. Your clothing was free, plus many things that were controlled by the law of the kibbutz. It was claimed that a person on the kibbutz was given more entertainment than a person from the city. It may be so, but you're not really free in a sense that you can take off when you please. For many years, the kibbutz rejected anything that does not fit or is not any use to the kibbutz. That meant that people would leave because someone wanted to be a racing driver, for example.

For those people, it wasn't quiet in the middle of the day, the flat bang, right in the middle of the place where they started to remove the soil from the foundation. Well, the engineer left the kibbutz for the city, finding it hard to cope that he was the guy who spent all those years in school to learn how to solve the problem, etc. Expert knowledge would be overturned by these people voting in ignorance; it didn't make sense.

So, who or what is the kibbutz good for?
Though many came and went, the kibbutz is good for many kinds of people, like those that can't really make it on the outside economically, and those that have to be in a group. The real reasons why so many came here? The Americans because of Korea, others because they felt they wanted to try something new. Many of the Israelis joined because they were in the Nahal Youth, meaning that since they could not afford an education, their parents put them in a kibbutz at the age of 14. To some of them it was good because they learnt half day plus worked, so when they come out of the army, they would be a member. Yes, each one had their reason for being there, but for the most it was not for idealist reasons. The Nahal Youth for teenagers fed the Israeli Defence Force [IDF] Nahal brigade. For this, like I said, the Americans thought that they were better than the others. The other groups were not any better; in fact, I was an outsider. Today, things have not changed this much. I'm still a proud outsider.

> *I am also a proud outsider. Started at age four, when adults believed in the weird concept of an afternoon rest. I preferred running round arms outstretched as a aeroplane.*

The whole idea of kibbutz life is good for those that do not want pressures of money, or any responsibility. It was nice, even great, but after a while you became bored, frustrated. Seeing the seasons go by, a better harvest, another building entered sometimes in the wrong area of the kibbutz, like the swimming pool. Life on a kibbutz is great for kids. They get everything, *an education*, and if they don't like their parents, they just don't go to them. One such kid adopted me for a week.

Kids were always adopting Jacques, like moths to a flame.

Using people's talents
For many years the kibbutz rejected anything that does not fit or is not any use to the kibbutz. There was a man there that was so very good at managing the economy of the kibbutz that they refused to let him step down, so they kept voting him back to this job. What happened in the end was that he made an ultimatum by saying that he did not want that job any more and if he was voted in again, that he would leave. He left. He was a very good man, he was a leader without even trying, a very good talker, too. Like I said, in a group there are a lot of people that can't stand each other, but they live together. Maybe it's the fight: I'm better than you, or the ideas that they don't like.

One of my favourite stories is the swimming pool. The man that knew more about and planned it, brought it up to the members, detailed all the reasons, why he wanted it on the outer boundary of the kibbutz. Lieb Shinness was the engineer, full of degrees, wonderful singer, etc., and too civilised. The majority were against his plan because it would be too far away from the houses where people lived. Since we live in an A-bomb age, it would be much better to have **it** near the centre. So, it would be a laundry one side, the cow shed and the storeroom; it would be very cramped. Lieb was thinking of the future and not of today, but that the housing would probably one day reach the pool. What he said was logical, but they did not want to know. He gave up trying to explain his point. It is very rare to see a city or village designed the right way. Some people there have never wandered out of the kibbutz more than a mile. Like in the city, there are people that have crossed seas or even Timbuktu, but to go down some side street – that is too much. The advice of the engineer was turned down, by a vote of individuals that didn't understand the situation.

Becoming a member
I was just made a member, like a marriage. The chairman said, 'Is there any reason why you shouldn't become a member?' There was no reason, and I was voted in. Now I had the right to vote, I could start by advancing in the power of people through the meeting conference, but my mind was not ready to do this; the daily routine was getting too boring for me.

Kibbutz economy
It took a long time for the kibbutzim to go into industry, especially as the Israeli economy was English style. A bad thing for the kibbutz, because they refused to invest, or modernise, do what you have to, etc. Like we grew too many things that needed labour. Also, farming on this scale, you have the human factor: this one does not want to work with that – it is like a kindergarten. The poor chap that does the planning for everyone that has to put the chap in this area has also to make sure there is no friction. In the short period of my stay in 'Kiss of Fire', I saw more than meets the eye. As long as you put your eight hours in, you're all right; but if not, then you have had it. There was the guy from Brazil with 10 languages behind him, a loudmouth who did not work right. He went from one job to another, he never settled. It did not help him that he had all those languages.

> *Jacques is writing about 1956. Now, in 2022, and for many years, kibbutzim barely exist. They are now mostly tourist resorts and are investment companies, with some communal ownership. Key assets like houses (and cars) are owned individually, not communally. More John Lewis than Jacques Rousseau. Socialism is conspicuous by its absence.*

1956 War
Oh, yes, I forgot it was the 1956 War during this time. The war was three days old; due to a misunderstanding, I did not know it was on. It's amazing, when there is war, everybody is digging trenches, and on guard duty, and

it looks like it is the end of the world. The 1956 war was between digging holes in the ground and getting yelled at by that Mordehai. Every night at the Ministry of Labour he would yell his head off, saying that he could not work with me because of the language, that I was a lazy bastard, but it did not help him, he was stuck with me. Can you imagine the funny noises that were supposed to be someone trying to tell me how I was supposed to lay down irrigation pipes? Many years later, I realised that he did this to show that he was the boss and don't forget it.

Amazing how 'incidental' the 1956 war is in this Nahal kibbutz.

Kissufim characters and incidents

During my year in 'Kiss of Fire', many things happened – like that short 1956 war. I put them in order so that you will be more amused at this mixed-up lot. My first account is of being in a group that I shall call a mini-nation of people, not more than 153 working on projects with all the peaceful world of landscape and silence.

Toby Soulan and the wagon incident

The wildest of them all was Toby Soulan. He was in trouble again. It was said about him that he had a very bad experience from the Germans during the Second World War. Yet this man had no fear when you went on patrol through the fields at night. I was stunned! He just walked like he was in the limelight of London. Well, this chap couldn't work with anybody – he would drive anybody up a tree – so they gave him a wagon and mule, and he would deliver the milk, eggs, and the meat, etc. I can remember it just like yesterday. He came in the dining room, sat down at the table where I was eating and started to talk. When he started, there was no way you could do anything. You know, he said, 'It's only 12 noon and the mule ran off with the wagon.' On it was a case of eggs, probably 24 dozen, six cans of milk and an empty bottle. Well, by the time he stopped, everything flowing in all directions on coming back to the kitchen, it went over two water mains. So, here I am; in every group is a joker like Toby or better.

Maverick: A memoir of Jacques Kornbrot, 1938 - 2014

Pig incident

Agriculture was the main thing that brought in most of the money, with the milking cows. We even tried our hands breeding pigs. Unfortunately, Americans that were visiting started a killing round up, as the pigs were not kosher. Meanwhile, dear young Toby was trying to catch them. These wonderful few that probably ate pork chops at home, suddenly became religious and told us if we didn't get rid of them, they would stop sending us American dollars. So, for the next four days we were feasting on pig breakfast, lunch, dinner; that was the last time we were to eat in such style.

Mordehai the Yemenite: shooting affair, Arabs, pipe theft

My next job was with a Yemenite called Mordehai; he was a son of a bitch. He could not understand that I did not understand what the hell he wanted me to do. It made him furious, after a while, seeing that Mordehai's group was not getting along with the rest of the others.

The other best instance was the shooting affair, also of a yelling boss. I was doing guard duty one night, in the light tower. With me was Mordehai. Every 10 minutes or so we would switch on the projector, like a prison camp. We would go around the field, watching if our neighbours, the Arabs, were not stealing irrigation pipelines. They were good at this. It was rare that we caught any of them. I switched on the light and started our Stalag 17 act. We saw someone walking towards the border with something shining like a pipe. We yelled. I went down from the tower, yelled again; no reply, bang, I fired to scare them off. Missed!

Then out there this voice was yelling like a mad man, 'Stop firing!' To me it still looked like someone going off with an irrigation pipe, whatever anyone said. He slowly came towards me. I reloaded, carefully walked towards him. You'd never know it was this other man who always found something to yell about. Though he was half-German, half-English, he had picked the Middle East disease of yelling – or, better, oriental. It's normal to yell.

Moshe Herzberg's first words to me were, 'Who gave you permission to shoot at me?'

I felt like shooting him for that question. He went under the tower without telling anyone that he was going out to the field to change the night lights on the tractor. It was the first time that someone fired at him, but that's another story. Daybreak came, and I went back to my room to sleep. Boy, did I feel miserable for the next few days. Some of the others took the mickey by saying I was a bad shot. It's not every day that one gets to take a shot at someone you know. What good came out of it was that he never did yell at me again, and we became the best of friends. A blessing from my shot.

> Jacques could always see the bright side! He often made friends where the initial meet was bad!

Planting the vines
When everybody is busy doing something, then things change, like the planting of the vines. One night, the Arabs formed on the other side crossed and took them out, and probably replanted them in the Gaza Strip. So, there was gossip going about two days, then we replanted and guarded that field. I guess they thought twice about doing what they had done two nights before.

Gaza Strip
Many of us went to see the Gaza Strip and the Sinai desert. Only an idiot would spend 40 years in it. They say it was because they were studying that they forgot what they really were there for. The Strip looked very poor; indeed, the poverty there was beyond one's imagination. More than a thousand were still ploughing, using the old ways, four-inch deep, pulled by a camel. As for those lands, quite fertile, they still use the method of leaving the weeds that attract the dew. Though the Egyptians were there for quite a time, they didn't do much to advance the people's needs. Like everything or any nation that conquers, it does very little to bring the

conquered to modern times. We hiked through the place and the Arabs were ready to sell the resistance people to us for cigarettes. I wonder, if I was put in that situation, I would do likewise? Alas, I have never been in that situation.

> *Jacques, as always, understood the others' point of view. What Jacques saw before Israelis pulled out in 2005 was bad, but later it was much worse. Israelis voted for that. Since 7th October 2023, Gaza (led by Hamas) is at all-out war with Israel.Kissufim was a amjor target in 2023 massacre.*

At night, we stayed with the (Israeli occupying) soldiers, and they were not too happy to sit there doing anything crazy but guarding major stores. One was loaded with a million blankets and the other one rice, and you won't believe this, halva as far as the eye can see, food galore. We continued through Sinai and finally arrived at the Suez. It was the second time that I have seen it, once when I went through on my way to Israel and now from land.

I don't think that I was proud ever of being one of those chosen few or even belonging to a group of people that didn't see further than their noses. We were lucky and got a lift right back to the 'Kiss of Fire'. The place was not changed, as we were only away four days. It was like going a thousand back in the same place. Like Rafah, if you would take away the electricity and water, you would be back in the time of the Romans, or even further back.

Back to normal
Slowly, things got back to normal. Many people came from Chile and other South American countries to help out. They were really a laugh. Most of them did not understand any of my languages; each came for different things: like divorce, etc., searching for a new kind of life. The atmosphere of life in a commune. They were called Sa-Hram; from their original group of 80, two stayed, maybe on the kibbutz. The rest went

back or went to the city. Kibbutz life, like I said, in those day had limitation of freedom of what you wanted to do. You are secured, but you have to follow and remain in the framework of the kibbutz. You just can't take off and do what you want. As far as I could see, the limitation is that it is only the few that rule the rest. What I mean is, you can have all people capable to be the leader, but someone has to follow orders, or it won't work. So, this quote of equality, liberty, the beautiful brotherhood, does not exist in any society. Those that think they can search that will find himself alone in the end.

Getting seconded to Eilot

The season dragged on. I was starting to get bored there and my youth, I guess, was getting the better of me. At the time, I was working in the production growing wheat, corn, ploughing the fields, feeding them with chemicals and manure. It was great: one man, one machine, ripping up the soil. I said to the head manager that I applied for the job, and he said, 'Oh, that's all right.' He didn't mind. So, I started to search about what next.

Then, one day, they wanted someone to replace someone that was in Eilot, creating a new kibbutz situated right in Eilat near the sea. (It is a bit confusing that the Kibbutz is Eil*ot*, but the town is Eil*at*).The main kibbutz produce, and money-makers were fishing, a welding shop, a laundry and keeping dates for the Ministry of Agriculture. Also, once a month, they went into the hills to fill bags of white sand that a kind of glass was made out of. I went to the chairman of the kibbutz and volunteered. He replied that he would bring it up to the meeting on Saturday night. The big night arrived for the Saturday conference where the chairman was going to bring it up. The show would begin. But first they went through what happened during that week, economically speaking, and there was not much new in that field. Just that it might be possible to build a few more houses with toilet and shower, because in those days you only had a room that would be shared. I even found myself in one room with three people for a month. We asked the chairman continuously and said that we were now able to relieve our man in Eilot with a substitute, and that I had asked the chairman to be put under consideration, if nobody else wanted to go. Since I was not yet a member of the kibbutz, I had the last call. Then, from nowhere, people were saying that I was young and what could I do there since everybody sent down there was 10 years older than me. My head foreman that had said early in the week that didn't matter, suddenly got up and said that Eilot had nothing to give to me and I should stay here. I felt like I was double-crossed. He could have told me his thoughts. I might have changed my mind, but this conference was more for accepting his point of view. It was well known that most of the people that went down there were having a hard time in getting married. So, from many kibbutzim, they send down many of these, hoping they would find a suitable partner. Since I was 18, they thought it would be bad for me. Moshe, the man I took a shot at, was the worst. 'It is a crime that we have to send me to go down to a place where he will be the youngest,' he said with seriousness. I did not know he cared that much. Suddenly, I felt important, like if I left, the whole place would fall apart. Not in the history of my life did I feel so wanted, by so many. I think it was the first time in my life I felt wanted by a group.

What a reflection on his life that it was the first time.

The chairman got up and said, 'You people don't want him to go. Good. Then if none of you want to go, then we shall have to find somebody that will,' and he added that now they would vote whether Jack should go or not. The voting started with all against. Moshe and some others still thought I should stay. I thought, 'Well, there goes my adventure trip.' So, they finally came to their senses, because otherwise they would have got a list; then they would have someone to go down whether they liked it or not, because that is how democracy works. Unless there is someone that wants to go, they appoint someone. So then those that were afraid to be sent down voted for me to go. I won by a majority.

CHAPTER 8: JACQUES' WRITINGS: ISRAEL, 1956-1972

I went to Eilat, the land of sunshine, sand, desert, to build a new kibbutz near the sea, the Red Sea.

Kibbutz Eilot

Arrival at Eilot

I got my little suitcase ready and off I went to the area of many mountains which are Mount Sinai. When the Red Sea is still, there is no wind or an inch of air. The reflection turns the sea dark brown, and the coral comes out to play. On my arrival, I was introduced to everybody and shown where I was to sleep. I unpacked.

Then I went straight into the sea for a swim. Damn Israelis, they did not tell me that you had to wear running shoes. My feet were greeted by those very prickly things, the ones that lodge in your feet. As it happened, they would stay there forever; man, was I in pain! I came out while some of them were watching me, waiting for me to yell my head off, but I kept my cool.

Since there was a limitation of my Hebrew, I asked if there was a first-aid kit. The dining room, that was large for the amount of people we were, had a cupboard with all the medicine one could think of. Fisher, as he was called, looked at my sole and said they would never come out; they would slowly disappear into the blood stream. Then he took out the funny-shaped glass tube, shook it, then sprayed the wound, if one can call it that. It was cool and the pain went away for ten minutes; then I just had to live with that pain for a few more days.

That was my welcoming to the Gulf of Aqaba! Was I in pain for a few days? There were no signs to say beware or be careful. Yes, I have always found out the hard way. I have learnt since, never trust anybody when going in dark houses or crossing the road; but I do forget sometimes, and land myself in it again.

Maverick: A memoir of Jacques Kornbrot, 1938 - 2014

Eilot kibbutz living

In 1957, in the Wild West of Eilat, I learnt a lot of things. About fishing, palm dates, laundry, welding, cooking. It was very peaceful there, even though we were boxed into the profession of fishing. It was like a bathtub, but we did make a fortune on the fish – when it turned up.

We were a group of 19: 15 men and four women – one was maybe in her fifties, and I had the pleasure to share the same room as her and another guy. She adopted him like her son; she used to make his bed. They said she lost her husband in 1948 – and her son in the 1956 war. I must have slept in the room for quite a time before I moved to another room. It was funny.

Well, the kibbutz was in a U-shape. If you were in the air, we were right in the line of planes landing or taking off, and it would disturb me every night when I fell asleep. I never got used to this. The men were all members of different kibbutzim. Most of them were sent by their kibbutz, because once a bachelor passed a certain age, to find a wife was very hard. I was the youngest of all. It was a very pleasant atmosphere. We took it in turns to cook and maintain the kibbutz.

At dinner, everybody sat round the U-shaped table, and could see each other and what they were eating, and even if they were in a good mood or not. The age was from 25, up to 65 years old, and I was really the youngster. Even though, till this day, they claim that women outnumber the men by 5 to 1, where the hell do they hide them? In all my travel in the world I have always been where there were more men than women, so something's wrong somewhere.

Men are more likely to travel!

Relaxing

After supper, we would go out and sit on the lawn and look towards Aqaba with its few lights, and relax after the big meal of fish, cooked, smoked and salad, forget the wine.

The place felt very deserted; the welding shop, laundry, the 200 dunim date fields were unworked for weeks. (1 dunam, plural, dunim is 1000 square feet). The date plantation was right on the Jordan border. We would cross it for a minute, then jump back to Israel. The only signs of the frontier were barrels: the border guards used to move them into Jordan a couple of feet, then the Jordanian patrol would put them back. I don't really know if they were the right boundary. A million years ago, the ocean reached right to the Dead Sea near Beersheba. The mountain or hills are covered with sharks in the chalk. If you used a chisel and hammer away where there were grey spots in the chalk – and, of course, finding the right end of the chalk – you might find its teeth and other rare fossils of a sort.

Building a kibbutz

That year I spent in Eilat building up a kibbutz from zero was more than joy. The Gulf of Aqaba, with its mountains of dark brown, when the sea is still the sea, turned to red. Yes, yes, what a place! Clean, a very dry climate – and a very sleepy place.

Every day there was something new that turned up. I wasn't any more in the midst of the people of Kissufim, who were more in the field of verbal work than anything else. Yes, at Kissufim there were too many educated ones, and a very small percentage that would really work. The Eilot kibbutz was always in the red! Eilat for me was good; for one thing, my Hebrew improved, and I could get a conversation, though I was told that the Israelis didn't speak the correct way. Still, no one there spoke any other language but Hebrew. It was quite depressing when we sat down at a table to eat, and you couldn't understand what your neighbours were saying.

The kibbutz life was good. You had five places you could choose from, and my favourites were the date tree, and the watching of the fish.

Kibbutz economy

We lived off a welding shop; we had in town a laundry, and fishing nets on the shore of Eilat. The fishing was great. Mostly it was tropical, with the net full out, circling an area, and once the fish were in the net, we would close it by pulling it in, whether it was full or not. You were pulling 10 tonnes. It made anybody that was weak pretty powerful. After a while, I got quite good at forcing the net using the big toe on my left foot and becoming a lever. A shark would destroy the net by getting himself entangled. If it weighed over 30kg, we would sell it for fish food; but it if was under, we would have shark steak.

Supplied by the kibbutz

Oh, yes, we were building a kibbutz. You know, at the end of the month they gave you 10/- to spend. You got food, clothing, a meal the communist way – not the Russian communist way. My Hebrew was very weak. Gunter and me were the only non-Israelis, except our fishing mentors, the Italian lecturer and the Jap who had a Ph.D. in fishery. Between the welding and growing dates and the laundry, we made quite a good living.

The plantation and its risks: locusts

Our plantation of dates was very young, maybe five or six years old, and we tried to grow wheat and barley, but failed. There was too much salt in the soil; all one had was to dig six feet and you would reach a spring. There were some areas where you didn't need even to dig. It was muddy and very uncomfortable, and if you were there with bare feet with cuts, you would hurt like mad.

It was very interesting how one plants a date tree: you dig a hole four by four metres and two metres deep. In the first year, you have to water every two weeks. Even that is getting some of the nourishment from the spring. Once it gives fruit, it continues for a hundred years. Working in the plantation was fun and repeating every two weeks you had to water them, then spray them for disease; even that that they were embedded on a salted spring, that did not affect the date tree. All those dates on palms you have in Eilat were taken care of by us, though it belonged to the Ministry of Agriculture. Today, the trees are giant. As for work, being a fisherman, I didn't wait the 10 or 15 years to taste them if they were good or bad. Whereas, as a date grower, I struggled between feeding them and fighting for their lives against the locust and the Bedouin from stealing the water taps!

- Well, today, when I go down there and look at the plantation, I feel I did my bit to create something to give pleasure to the birds and people's stomachs.

A real positive! The kibbutz itself is now well inland.

The worst disaster that happened for it was the locust, since all of us were greenhorns on the subjects of the locusts. With all our knowledge of disease, we thought that the red ones were harmless, for the yellow ones laid their eggs. But as for the locust, it was more damaging than the Bedouin. Just nobody knew that the red locust is more destructive than the yellow one. The Ministry of Agriculture sent planes to spray them. The road going out of Eilat was loaded with locusts for mile and miles. They did not kill the plants. Well, it was a couple of months since the whole Middle East had an agreement that when the pest start their immigration, it is wired to everybody in the neighbourhood, like the weather. It was warned by all countries; after that, no one loved anybody between Israelis and Arabs.

There was an alert on Thursday that they were coming from the Sudan by the millions and we had to prepare ourselves with stick noises to scare them away with the help of the army and anyone we could muster. They were the yellow ones that lay eggs. These, according to the experts, were the dangerous ones. So, a spray plane came down, stopping their flight. But some got through and headed north. Damage was not that bad; they apparently lay their eggs in the sand, them move on to better places, and so on.

The locust this time were red, dark red, and the experts said that it was dangerous to the plants. Those little insects knew when to come – on Friday afternoon, as Saturday is the day of rest. Well, when we came on Sunday morning, they had eaten the leaves away and the branches were bare; that meant that fruit would be delayed by two to three years. It is amazing that with all the information, and the expert that was on the spot, we did not know about this horrible pest. This backlash must have set back the date plant tree three to four years of growth. They came in a million or more.

FishingThen there was the fishing, which was most of the time lying on the beach and waiting for them to come into the gulf and trap them in the net or surround them, then throwing the net in. The tutor was an Italian that the kibbutz had hired to teach us all there is to know about nets mending them, plus in which area the places were for the catch.

We had a couple of small motorboats plus three rowing boats. Every day we would go around the net and see through a converted pot with a glass bottom if there were any fish caught in the net. This was done by one rowing around the net, then checking everything was all right. Then we would be sitting about, like reading or talking. Then we got a pulley to draw in the nets.

The catches were small and large. In the period that I was a fisherman there, rowing as physical work, one would imagine that I would produce muscles. Not one decent health muscle, but I got good at rowing. Nemo, the Italian instructor, told me that his yelling at me was not personal so that I should not get angry at him. It was the manner of the way that fishermen handle things. The way he had just finished telling this, he started to yell in his native tongue, with hands and feet, mixed with his poor Hebrew. It might sound funny, but by Christ he was a bastard.

We made a small catch, then you go to the shore and pull in the nets, everything going right, everybody in sight giving a hand. He is yelling like a wild gorilla. Suddenly, he yells, 'Dai', which in Hebrew is enough. We all let go, and the only person to hold the net is dear Nemo. The net was slowly going back into the sea, opening up a gap, and the fish got away scot free. Boy, was he hopping mad! He cursed everyone that was near him. One of the Israelis said, 'But you gave an order to stop.' Ten guys stood with their mouths open at that, including me. Of course, I kept a serious face from him. But he continued, not wanting to know anything about who was right. We let him down, and to him that was a crime. It would be the first or last time that happened again, but in a different way. Nemo could never understand that there were people weaker than himself. He thought that everybody had the same strength. He was a big man from Sardinia, and he did not look like any Italian. He could have passed as a Scandinavian, because of his blond hair, but once he opened up his mouth, he was an Italian. He taught me how to fix nets and catch fish, plus yell; even though there was a mix of languages between us, we got along fine.

Our Italian instructor didn't like the way we were trying for the catch. Tuna catching is a very delicate job of its kind. Since it was a very expensive way to catch tuna by nets, it would rip them apart without much strain. Once the long line of rope was held up by the buoys, the tricky returning was not easy; the schooner we had was not made to go alongside. How the Italian fishes, or Nemo as is he was called, intended to come ahead on the rope went along side and caught the equipment in the rope. What a mess; it made a disaster. We had to dive down and cut it free, and it wasn't easy. The rope was dipped in bitumen as it would be longer than without it. We got everything working again, but the only thing we ever caught was shark and no tuna. After a few months, the Japanese pro said farewell, and that was the last time we ever tried to change our method of fishing.

> *Apparently, they had Japanese and Italian experts at the same time, and they did not agree!*

He could not understand that there were other people that were not as strong as himself. He once was in the boat fishing and caught a 120kg Ten guys stood with their mouths open at that, including me. Of course, I kept a serious face from him. I learned how to row; after a while I was great. You would think my muscles grew like a bodybuilder's; well you are all wrong – I stayed the same.

We caught a shark Nemo battled with it for four hours – the shark was pulling him in one direction and he was rowing like mad in the other direction – he literally was rowing on the spot. We watched from the shore. When he came in with his catch, he looked exhausted.

We even went as far too long after the fish itself, since the season of the fishermen was short. Then it was decided that we would do tuna fishing, which is quite a delicate way of fishing because they are rather long and very strong. Each time there were a few about, it would take us four or five nets to catch them. So, a Japanese expert was brought in. He had beside that a Ph.D. in fishery, and it made Nemo jealous.

We had to get a rope that would be laid out flat on the sea. Every 10 metres was a float to keep the rope up, and in between was a hook with a sardine, so for and so on. Right then, all you had to do was to come the next day close to the rope and check whether you had made a catch or not. It was very tricky indeed. With the winch you pulled it up. It was there we got sloppy about it and got the rope stuck in the propeller. Some say it was dear Nemo, some say nobody took watch. Hence, the idea of having it in the little bay or bathtub, as the Jap called it.

We went further out into the Red Sea, and the fishing there was even worse. They caught more shark than anything else. That was a bad investment, so that little schooner was laid up. Thank God for that. I hated starting it. You would have these candles with gunpowder on the end and plug them into the piston. That part was all right, but you had to crank it; and believe me, two people used to come out with sore heads because the place it was in, it was impossible to move far enough out of the way without hurting some of your body. Mostly, it was the head or chest. Then we got better equipment, but saving about eight to nine manual hands, but to start the engine you still had to do it by hand. Well, after having been fed a Japanese meal of raw tuna with lemon, the Jap departed back to Japan and Nemo felt happy again, saying the man was useless.

We once caught a 10-tonner. A crane was brought in to bring it out. What a night. The things we would find in its stomach: shoes, beer bottles, radio, hair dye. According to people that research on sharks, they do this as they can stabilise themselves while swimming. Crazy, I admit to say, but amazing how useful this information would be. Find a shark that's off balance and you catch it just like that.

Most of the fishes which were caught in the spring, two months of running like mad. Once we had the net show with a catch inside, outside was another large school of them. I jumped in the boat with Nemo, our Italian instructor, and we rowed like the electricity current. I continued for now, Nemo throwing in the nets, circling them without disturbing them, and we had caught about 25 tonnes of palamida. Then came the hard work of dragging in the net. We must have worked for about an hour without stopping for a rest. Once we had them in cases, we drove to the deep freeze, stacking them up till there was no more room in the place. Then rushing back to catch, dragging the net again. Man, when we finished, about two o'clock, the girls had made enough food to drown an army, with all the trimmings.

Palamida was the main catch. Seems to be a kind of tuna.

Maverick: A memoir of Jacques Kornbrot, 1938 - 2014

On one occasion, in one period of 16 hours, we made a large catch that must have been worth a fortune. We had to pack them in boxes, and that took a long time. Everything was closed up, 15 of us working like mad, transporting everything to the freezing plant. We must have had over 10 tonnes of palamida. Each net was brought into pack, and this continued till there were no more fish in the large net. With only a few hours to daylight, we went into the dining room. It was loaded with food on the table no one had the strength of eating.

We just looked at it and we all turned in to the large room we all slept in at the time. I find that when I work that hard, it is very difficult to fall asleep quickly. So, while everybody was snoring their heads away, suddenly Uri yelled out, 'Fisher, Fisher!'

Everybody was waking and probably saying to themselves, 'Shit, it is already morning!' Some were already putting on their shoes to go, when I said he had been dreaming again. Most of them moaned something about that son of a bitch.

Never have I seen a group of people that could get so much sleep as after this catch. One guy averaged about 18 hours of sleep, non-stop. For myself, I was up early, hoping we might get another catch; but due to the commotion, the other school of fish probably didn't come into the gulf. It was quiet for another week, and we caught a tonne right when the fishermen in the Med had a bad catch. We got about four times the value of the catch. Sometimes, because there were so many fish, it was worth more selling as a fertiliser, or animal feed.

We would have been millionaires at the time. The fishing fleet in the Mediterranean had a very bad catch, and the prices were very high indeed – something like a million at today's rate – but we did not see a penny of it. It all went to the head of the kibbutz clan in Tel Aviv.

Group organization, socialism?

Cooking

From the whole group there wasn't any envy about who was going to be whom. We all did what we had to do in work. In the evening, we would rotate who was going to fix the meal. When my turn came, I asked if it would be possible for me to make steak and eggs, since in those days steak was a delicacy for anybody and was very expensive. Since we were millionaires in a sense, while most of the excess money we made went straight to the head of the kibbutz or a special bank account for the future of the kibbutz. Everybody agreed that I would make the steak and chips, of course. I put on an apron and sang 'Malaguena'. Very diplomatically, I said, 'Do you want medium rare or well done?'

Everybody said, 'Since you're from Australia, make it the way you would make it there.'

So off I went to the kitchen, singing my 'Malaguena', which in those days was my favourite song. I nearly got to such perfection, that one of the girls coming in said she thought it was the radio. I assured her that it was me singing it. Ha, what a laugh.

When I took the plate in with the steak, one poor man cut it and saw blood coming out. He rushed back to me and said in a furious tone, 'I want mine fried through.'

Well, that was that; they all had it fried through. What would you expect? It was nice sitting.there, a small family with hardly any care, except that most of them were supposed to find a man or a woman. If I recall, there was one married couple that came down from Givat Brennner. They were nice, even younger than me, I think, but I'm not sure.

Daily life
So, spending my working days between the laundry and catching fish and planting date trees, life moved on slowly, meeting a lot of people from all over the world that came to Eilat, from paupers to the commander of the sixth fleet. After talking with him and his aide, he nearly crossed the border, but was caught in time. Even one of the Rothschilds came – but did not contribute to the kibbutz. We had also the first hydroponica there that produced our tomatoes, peppers, and eggplants. We tried experiments with all sorts of plants which would grow below; those grown two to three metres below, where there lay spring water with quite a bit of salt, with which we watered the date tree and tried the other plants to take, but it was only without being worth to grow because the seeds were of a very poor quality. Now, when I pass the area and see those date trees there three times my height, I feel proud that more than 20 years ago I helped to dig those trenches for them.

Let's get back to the routine of the kibbutz. As people finished their year and went back to their kibbutz, others came. Those that were still there took the responsibility of chairman and accountancy. Thanks to my character, I would probably have made a bad chairman and accountant. I stuck to the routine of the fishing, plantation, laundry, but most of it was with the fishing.

Current situation of socialism?
Today, nearly 20 years later, it has not worked the way the old timers thought it would. It has become more a money-making enterprise than anything else. It is not that easy a life, work or to have enough food for what you need. It is more the ideals that are different. Marxist Leninism does not exist there any more. In my eyes it is a very well-organised structure for big groups to be able to live together, each giving what they had. In China, they have 70,000 people in one commune. It would be great to know if there are any differences.

CHAPTER 8: JACQUES' WRITINGS: ISRAEL, 1956-1972

Now we know about China! Centralised capitalism. Massive repression and racism. Social inequity. No starvation?

Real-life communal/communist experience
One has to be on the spot to really know, rather than to read it in books. The practice is more important. By the book, things only work if it is a replacement of one or two items; but if you try to change a complete field of one thing that should work, then you are in a mess, due to things like, not everybody likes to be told what they are supposed to do. There must be something that balances out, on both sides.

Today, there are not many idealists. I believe that you could have left that kibbutz in Eilat, in the position where it was. It would have been an experience to see if you could have a large group among the city sharing its wealth. On small scales, as in Denmark, it works. Even in America they have the communes. Eilat city had 4000 people at the time, and slowly more people were coming down there. Hotels were being built and more and more tourists were coming down to Eilat. It was a good training ground for me, seeing how people live in groups of tens or twenty or three. That is how many we had left.

Social and 'romantic' life
My Hebrew improved there because there were not many Israelis that understood anything but Hebrew. So, it did not take a long time for me to get going in that language; that as a way for women, and men for the third sex, does not exist (Jacques does not seem to have been aware of any 'third' sex in Eilat). The days were pleasant. The period I was in Eilat, I learned a lot of things like politics, laundry, fishing, and a new form of growing in stone and not to get drunk in the summer – that was a killer. Being drunk and having a cold was even worse; being the youngest there had its disadvantages. The few girls that were there were not wanting to go to bed, but to get married. I had to do my best on the outside tourist girls coming down for the weekend. Where are all those girls...?

Jewish festivals

For the Jewish festivals, it was quiet. Me and Gunter decided that we would get dressed up and have a ball, but the others didn't go for it. Gunter dressed himself as a baby and he made a pottie. Inside he made, I mean he got a banana and coated it with chocolate, and poured a pint of beer, and walked in and started to eat and drink it. Everybody just watched and did not find it funny or anything. I came running in as the mama and took him out. That was Purim for you: besides getting drunk and chasing women there and reading books and saying that communism will never work.

Tourist visitors

Like I said, while waiting down on the beach for the fish to come, we talked to the few tourists that used to come down there. Also, women by the bagful used to come down there, especially those that had just got divorced, who came down to recuperate and pep up their sex life. So, if you had the patience of being a good listener, or charm, you had yourself one good evening. Nemo was good at this; his mediterranean training gave him first pick. I went for the not crazy ones that were searching for the rainbow, just for the sake of sex.

International visitors

We had many interesting people coming down to Eilat, some coming from Africa by boat as far as Iran, and Australia raising sheep, and the most important wealth: oil from Iran.

Yes, one could meet on the seashore anyone from seamen to admiral of the American fleet, or the Baron De Rothschild, but he didn't donate any funds for the newly built kibbutz. We did get a motion projector from a group in Canada. We went to meet Mr Sweetapple in the only hotel, with Gershon and my roommate Dov. While they were breaking themselves within the English language, I was tasting the cool beer.

Then I broke into the conversation. The elderly man turned around, saying, 'You speak very good English.'

I replied, 'Yes. I am from Australia.'

He didn't find it funny at all, trying to get a thing going with poor Dov and Gershon. We gave him more details about the new kibbutz and where we intended to be when we finally moved. He claimed that he belonged to a group, and that they wanted to give us a motion projector. One doesn't believe it till one sees it. Well, a couple of months later the projector arrived, and it was a very nice job. How did it make me feel? Excellent, good, fair, weak? In the end, it doesn't change anything, friends.

Aircraft carrier
In the early morning during 1958, an aircraft carrier came to the fort of Aquia – British, of course. There was a feeling of tension at the time. Jordan was in difficulty, and she asked Britain for help. The helicopter was coming back and forth, transporting everything to the shore, as they couldn't really dock. The fighter planes were supporting the landing. There were two planes in the air at all times – what noise! It was very hard for listening; one can't really do much when things move this way.

Eilot kibbutz members
Let me describe those 20 beautiful people. These Israelis don't drink, except tempo (beer). It disturbed my roommate there when I used to come in at night, drunk out of my mind. To compensate for this, I taught him to read; but still he would complain about it. Most of the members there were more idealistic than me – nearly all of them; well, nearly all.

Presumably in English.

Naan was a big man. He used to be the security officer of the place, and the head of the laundry there. It was fun working with him. At breakfast, he would pull out of his pocket a pair of ladies' underwear, saying out loud, of course, 'Hai, Rachel, you forgot it in my room!' and there would a boom of a laugh. She would try not being insulted because he could have been her father. The other guy was in his 60s with asthma, and he was there for the only reason that Eilat is very dry.

Habbracha was tall, very strong, and always found something that would make us laugh. When he arrived, the next day he was supposed to leave with the others to go to the plantation, but the group leader forgot to wake him up, so at breakfast he was told where the plantation was situated, because one could not see it from the road due to the fact the dates were buried two to three feet in the ground, as I mentioned before. So off he set, coming back an hour and a half later saying that he got as far as the mountain and past the road. Then, we rolled with laughter, as he had crossed the border and went to the mountain and came back without a scratch. Maybe the Jordanian soldiers were afraid because they would be dealing with a funny man. But he was a strong man: when we were piling those rocks, he could pick them up like they were bales of straw, till one day the one he picked up over his head broke in the middle and hit his head, knocking him out.

The last funny that happened to him was that while he was spraying the date tree, a Bedouin came from behind and touched his shoulder. He turned and saw this poor Bedouin dressed up. Habbracha fell into the trench, and the Arab gave his hand to help him out. From fear, Habbracha started to spray with the spray gun, and all the Arab wanted was to defect to the Israeli side. We were all characters in a sense that when you are in a group, some people really stick out.

Uri Brenner was a kibbutznik. He was a 200% communist, good old Uri. He worked with such zeal. He was a person that had no limits. He did not like Rossini, because he was a capitalist. He tried to convince all the kibbutz that we could better place our settlement right on the border of Aqaba. We even started to build a pier with barrels and rocks. It was a hard job equally; we had to anchor down the barrels for the bottom with those large posts. We got the pier 50 feet out to sea and nearly finished it. It needed only two feet to finish the top layer.

We had real characters down there. Uri's only comment to me was that I would never marry a kibbutznik because I was not made for the kibbutz. I did not disagree. He worked like a maniac; there was no limit. He was so involved with it, that he dreamt about it.

Our dear Uri dreamt about poles. In the middle of the night he would get out of bed and put poles in our sleeping room, and everybody woke up and watched without saying a word. He finally woke up in the middle of the room, smiled, then got back into bed.

The best came about two weeks later, when we went through the piles gathering rocks to make the pier between the Jordan and Israel border, between Eilat and Aqaba, which till this day is a house which is empty. Then, one night, dear Uri lifted himself up, crying out, 'The rocks are falling!'

The guys that were sleeping in the next bed woke up, saying out loud that truly nothing was falling. 'What are you talking about?' These funny incidents happened quite often. One of the lads even tried to get him talking while he was in his dreaming mood, but it did not get far enough – he would wake up, then grin, saying, 'Try next time.'

Uri had returned to his kibbutz, marrying someone from the other side of the fence. The kibbutz was split in half in political thought. It goes to show, with all their ideas, they do marry 'out'. They say that they were given a house that was on the borderline of the kibbutz.

Then I lived for a while with Mahrun in the large room. He was a funny man; he used to get up in the morning and search on the ground for his toothbrush and toothpaste. I feel sort of angry with myself that I forbade him to drive the tractor because he did not have any experience. I should have known better. Maybe I was showing authority, something I dislike. You don't know anything. But we became good friends in the end. He would tell how the army forced him to become a commander, and they even cleaned his rifle, etc. He was born on a kibbutz.

There were also a few girls from there; and, mind you, I never touched any of them. They all looked at me as the baby, but that is another story.

At that time, I was living with an elderly lady that had lost her husband in 1948 and her son in 1956. She went round from place to place, helping out new settlements as a cook. There was the famous Dov, who she treated like her son. She would make his bed. On one occasion, it must have been two o'clock, when off she went that a girl was screaming her head off. The old lady said, 'Dov, go quick to see what is happening.' He replied, 'It is okay, she is only dreaming.' 'No,' said the elderly lady, 'she is probably getting raped.' So, we both went out and there were already a lot of people there handling the scene. Zev Gadol was there, saying she had one of her dreams again. Next to him was his double-barrel shotgun. He was looking not too happy – being woken up in the middle of the night is not a funny thing. So, we went back to bed, making the old lady happy.

So quite a few of them did not sleep easy in their beds.

I met her again many years later in an army camp. She recognised me, but I had not recognised her, and she yelled out in the middle of the dining room, 'Don't you remember, we lived together in the same room?' Oh, yes. I looked around and there were smiles and giggles all over the soldiers' faces, making me feel very uneasy. Yes, she was still going round helping out with the cooking.

A new boy, Gunter, came to us. He was German, and we ended up working together with Nemo, the Italian fish instructor. It was a laugh because of the language problem, but when one tries, everybody can make one understood. Nemo used to fool about. He caught an electric fish that had current, and he told Gunter to take that and throw it overboard. He picked it up and it shocked him all over.

There was David the Egyptian, with his sailboat, that got himself brought back by the Navy, speed boat, due he crossed the border and could not get back because of the wind – So they would bring him back half of the boat was under water...

Momo the monkey
There was also Momo the monkey, let us not forget him. He was the most hard-up monkey I have ever met; besides, he did not have a female partner. So, any woman that came around, he would go wild and want to touch them and would not let go at any price. We got him from a truck driver that used to go between Eilat and Tel Aviv. He literally lived in the truck's cabin, and in the big city he would blow the horn of the truck in the middle of the night or any time. Momo got that poor driver into trouble, so we bought him, and he was our mascot or recreation officer after work like a dog, but worse.

At the end of the day, we would sit on the lawn, bring Momo the monkey out and let him play about. As usual, he would find a way to unleash himself somehow, and he would take off to the sea that was just a few feet away. If there were not people there, we let him piddle about. There were always people trying their luck. Like the day we noticed this man walk up to him. Momo looked as the man bent to him, then grabbed the man's glasses, threw them away, jumped on his shoulder, pulling out his wallet, throwing the money out and starting to chew his plane ticket. He thought that that man would be able to handle him. No way. Like that poor girl that let him sit on her shoulder; he was fooling about with her hair, then got his hand entangled with her brassiere, yanking it out and ripping her shirt. She remained topless for a minute. In those days, even Eilat was prudish.

Maverick: A memoir of Jacques Kornbrot, 1938 - 2014

But the best was to come, when a football team came all the way from Beersheba. We took Momo along to see it. I don't remember exactly who was holding him, but he got away, ran straight for the ball, got it, and ran off in the direction of the airport. After him were 22 players. He finally let go of the ball and play went on again. We spent the afternoon searching for him, and found him in the kitchen, helping himself to the fruit and veg.

There are more stories about that monkey. Some of the things he did will make you laugh, but it was not funny at the time. When he got away during the day, he would rush over to the army canteen that was not far from us, and would jump over the counter. The people working there would run for their lives and come to us and tell us to get the monkey away. By the time we got to him, he had eaten two boxes of chocolate wafers. We paid, of course, and that was that till the next time. One of the best was when he ran towards the canteen. A policeman was sitting there drinking his beer when here comes Momo, and he grabs the bottle and finishes it. What annoyed the policeman was that it was not the fact that Momo drank it, but the fact that he just threw the bottle away and it broke. When you buy a bottle of any sort, you are charged, and you are refunded when you're finished. Besides that, he jumped over the counter and away. The salespeople ran for their lives again. Fortunately, there was one of us there at the time to get him out before he could taste any of the wafers.

Like I said, we had a lawn there and sometimes, when members of another kibbutz came down and asked if they could have a bed, we would put them up on the lawn in a sleeping bag. Well, dear Momo got out in the middle of the night and started to go through the guy's hair while he was still asleep, probably looking for fleas. Yes, sir, he was grooming the man, who woke up looking straight into the face of Momo, which is not something anybody would love to do. There was yelling and cursing from both sides. Momo was screaming and the guy was doing his bit. It took us two hours to catch Momo. When we finally caught him, he put both hands on his knee, *momomomomoo*, showing you that it hurt there. The game was that if you believed him, he then rushed you and took a bite; but if you were stern and gave him a good clip of the head, he would sort of cool down and go off to his cage.

> *Cage-building does not seem to have been a major talent on Eilot. Or they just did not like seeing any creature locked up – especially Jacques.*

Usually, when he got out, he would head straight to the girls' room, and if they have forgotten to latch the door or fly net, then they would be in for a surprise from Momo. When one yelled there, you would think that someone was being murdered, raped, or attacked by the whole Jordanian armed forces. There was one girl there that had bad dreams once a month; she would yell in such a manner that it would bring people from all over Eilat thinking something had happened.

The horniest monkey I ever met, he would find a way to get out of his cage to chase after women night or day, and he really kept at it. He would hop out from his cage in the middle of the night – and dash off to the girls' room. Then we would spend an hour catching him. On being caught, he thought that we were going to hit him, so he pretended that his knee was wounded; but if he knew you were afraid of him, he would take a big bite out of you. So, after a while, he knew who was who. Like a dog, he took five of them – but if it was just one, he would dash up a pole, then we would have a problem in catching him; but at the end he always gave in to food.

Army support and Bedouin camel incident
Even those date trees have a story to tell. Before we put up a 12-feet high fence it was open to the camels that would cross over from Aqaba to feed, and the Bedouin would take the brass tape off the mains at night. There must have been hundreds stolen by them. That is a story by itself. Work by day and work by night, we were given a platoon of soldiers, very active soldiers. We went into the area of the palm trees – and set

ambushes. Not to shoot them, but to catch them. There were two incidents – one was better than the other, and this all happened in the winter in the cold.

So, we got the army to do an ambush. The catch was that every night it would be someone else's turn to take them to the plantation and pick out a spot where to lay, and hope for the best the Bedouin would come near, and we could catch them red-handed. In those days I was pretty fast running, to what help it did when you are the hunter. Yes, sir, here I was the chief of one Israel lieutenant. and his happy men. They did not like the idea of catching them by hand. Later on, I found out that the soldiers were Druze and born fighters. The army would pick me up from the kibbutz. My dress was running shoes, one little pistol that I had never fired in anger, a couple of sandwiches, a flask of coffee. Off we went, me leading ahead of the column. It is amazing what happens when you walk in the direction of Aqaba: the light blinds you.

As we walked, you won't believe this, on the road we bumped into an Arab. The lieutenant that was behind me grabbed him by the belt. I was recovering from the shock of being bumped, but I could get over it. Two soldiers went back with him. I think he must have been a spy, because he was never mentioned again. There were nights out there that nearly drove me mad from how cold it got. I promise, if I caught one, I would push him into the sea.

Bedouin ambush and 200 camels.
Then, one clear night that you could see through binoculars, we saw what must have been some 200 camels coming nearer and nearer. They must have been a few feet away when the men gave such a yell and ran like mad after them. I took my target and went after him like the wind – what wind? The man disappeared into the darkness at such a speed, the Druze soldiers were saying and chatting among themselves. Then the sergeant came up to me and said, 'Give us permission to fire on them.' He said, 'My men are furious because one of them nearly had him by his

fingertip.' I replied, 'No way, you are here to catch them; they are just thieves, not soldiers like you.'

Jacques really did not like violence.

Suddenly, I realised we were stuck with 200 or more camels. Then, while I was trying to think, all of the camels pissed – they were great pissers. The sergeant kept giving orders to fire, but I said, 'In the air; maybe they will surrender just being shot in the air.' One could see the tracer going off and the camels just stood their ground. We did not have walkie-talkies. Then I said to the sergeant, 'Tell your radio man to report to your commander and ask what are we going to do with these animals?' He replied that they did not bring any radio.

In the meantime, as well as 200 camels, the three Arabs had left behind loads of hashish and a jacket that was made in Jaffa – that man really got around – and sandals made out of wheel tyres. Here I was with 12 angry men wanting to shoot those poor guys, and 200 camels. I turned round and told their leader that I was taking the driver and I would go to the headquarters and see what they wanted to do with all these camels, because I was lost for ideas. So, the driver and me took off. Before going, I told them not to move from the spot because we were coming back. Off we went back to the road, where the command car took us straight to the army headquarters. The first thing generals always say to you is, 'What are you doing here and how did you get through the camp?' I told him we drove there. Then I told him what happened and asked what should I do with 200 camels? He smiled at me, not believing that there were 200 camels, or more or less. He said, 'You go back, and I shall round up some men and will see what we can do.' We drove back this time to the edge of the plantation, then walked where they were supposed to be. No one there. 'Shit!' said the driver to me. 'Are you sure this is the spot?' I said, 'Yes, I know every inch of the area.' My feeling said to me, go back as fast as you can to the truck. We ran like I have never run in my life. We got into the truck, and I said to the driver, 'Start driving through those rows of dates.' We only went about 10 yards when two figures appeared with knives in hand. The sergeant, and the smallest in the lot, said to me, 'Did you see those two that ran your way like the wind?' I replied, 'Of course I did. Just him and me. You moved from the place I told you not to.'

This was 1957. Drugs were in use then; not like now, but these were dealers that crossed from Egypt through Israel to Jordan – and back. But we are still stuck with the camels. I said, 'If we all hide among them, they will probably think we have left, and then come to retrieve them, so we will catch them.'

The truck made a noise like they were leaving, and we started to rush the camels in the direction of the border. The camels started off beautifully; they started to spread out in the direction, and we let them go, watching through my field glasses.

> So, the 200 camels saved themselves and Jacques never saw them again.

Eilat and Aqaba were very quiet. No one shot at anybody. That was one of the reasons for the idea of catching them: they were just thieves making a small fortune from the brass. We finally had to build a fence 12 feet high – with a gate and a lock. I guess that they never broke in or finished the fence.

Jordanian problems: the Arab border with Aqaba

Due to the problem with the camels crossing from Aqaba to graze, they would, besides, eat their favourite plant on the salt plain and continue with the date trees, which were no higher than knee-high. So, we had to build a fence around. Hundreds of poles were put in, then barbed wire. Like this is peace except for the Bedouin that would come at night and steal the brass main. It still amazes me, the thought of two cities and all one could do is look at them through field glasses. I was still the youngest of the group, only my Hebrew was getting better all the time. The lobby of kibbutz were sending more people from different kibbutzim.

The scenery, living between two great mountains and three mountains which were not friendly, as our Japanese Prof of Fishery said, 'It's a bathtub!' The water, if I forgot and drank it, I would have the rum and would cross the border to the other side. There was a barrel that told you that you had a border; it said we moved towards them, and they would move it back! Whatever, it was peaceful down there. When I got there!

Some members crossed over to Jordan to visit Petra. Some came back, others were killed; one the way out, unless you went over the mountain, then you had more of a chance. But if you were lazy and went through the paths, you were doomed! Doomed!

Location of the kibbutz and ideology

Eilat had a port, with the presence of a frigate fishery boat, a sightseeing boat. Anyhow, the town was growing slowly. Many came and also many went their own way. We wanted to move the settlement to the Jordanian border away from the city. Then we were told that we would move the kibbutz a metre from Eilat. Right, but the city was approaching this point, and it wasn't far from the end of the runway. One would have planes over our head most of the day.

At one time, most of the people thought that the kibbutz would be staying, because the idea was to build the place on the border. It fell through. For a week we went on doing all the routine jobs. I was very naïve in those days. I must admit, if I was told we would move it to the moon, I would probably believe it.

Positioning the kibbutz?

The kibbutz movement leadership were really very serious people. This argument about where we were supposed to move brought down to us the elder Tabenkin, the famous known leader father of the kibbutz Ahdut HaAvoda, Moshe Carmel, plus that funny man Benny Marshak. Tabenkin started off with saying there will be cows and green fields and that it was impossible for the kibbutz to be built there. One guy from Givat Brennner said that he was just going to stay here till he was the last to go and take the fridge back with him. That's how much he thought of the matter. As for me, everything was translated.

Tabenkin said to Uri, 'How are things down here?' Uri replied, 'I'm only a tourist here.' That really made the old man mad. While he was giving us his point of view, he mentioned it like he had been betrayed. Slowly, Eilat grew and we knew that there was no way we were going to move to within a kilometre or the border between Aqaba and Eilat.

Kibbutz Central on location of kibbutz
The head officer of all the kibbutzim didn't like it; even better, it was political. The Government was thinking more ahead than us, by saying it would be stupid, because if peace should ever come here, the border would be opened and we would be in the way. The arguments were heavy, very sour indeed. As usual, the young Sabras revolted at the idea of it. In the meantime, we continued work, the laundry bringing in more wealth to control head office of the kibbutz in Tel Aviv. Financially, we were not doing too bad in the early days of the birth of Eilat with the port and the copper mine. The town was waking up after thousands of years of peaceful trading, and buildings were being erected all around us. Hotels and more hotels, with so many people coming down to Eilat, many running away from the north for hope and a new future. One of those people was a guy called Judah Bahrat, who brought down a schooner and named it *Calypso*. Those months that went by, it was like...

The communist Uri Bren was trying very hard to convince the head of the kibbutz offices in Tel Aviv that it would be good for us to be there because it was near the sea, and it would be out of the city of Eilat that was slowly growing at the time. The heads of all the kibbutzim said one kilometre from Eilat was going to be the spot, but the city was already half there anyway. So, we went ahead after working hour piling into the sea barrels of rock steel rods, the whole shooting match. We got about one metre under the water line, and we had to stop. We were forced to stop by the you-know-who.

We had a Mapam officer that came down and lectured us that there will be a kibbutz there one day somewhere some place – cow field etc. in the kibbutz, but we still wanted to build our kibbutz right on the border.

Communication: Kibbutz Central & Eilat Council
Then came word that we were refused permission to settle there. Mr Talbenkin, the Town Council and that ill-talking person Benny Marchak. They gave us a talk about why we couldn't settle down there. Mostly, the guy replied that it would be away from the city; Talbenkin saying there would be and there will be green fields about us. Since my Hebrew was limited, I couldn't follow most of it. Most of the faces here were very gloomy; no doubt no one there agreed with them, as it was political. The day will arrive that the border of Jordan – I mean Aqaba and Eilat – will be an open door.

Still waiting in 2024.

We started to build a pier – every Saturday we would load tonnes of rock and take it to the border where there was a green house, putting rock into the sea. We nearly reached 4.5 inches from the top of the sea, when we were told to stop by the head of kibbutzim. They came down to give us a lecture about it being unforgiveable to build the kibbutz right there, but we could build it somewhere else, like a kilometre from Eilat. The head office took our money and had discussions at the end of the day... politicians, of course! They are people who learn life by books and others learn by blood, sweat, toil. Most of what I know is from blood, sweat and toil. I have done as many things as possible, and nothing is sure or fell out on the hill of life. A couple of weeks followed and Uri, the top communist, went back to his kibbutz in the North; others followed till we were left with only four groups.

Fishing after location decision
Things were coming back to normal. The fishing was a very good income as we had a Japanese expert on our team to catch tuna. He gave a long Japanese whistle, whilst saying that it was a cloth tube. Fishing for tuna was done not with nets but with buoying a long rope on the surface of the water, then having a line going down four to five metres, with a hook and small fish as bait. The buoys could reach out for miles, but in Eilat we didn't have that much space at the time as we laid out about 500 metres. After this you wait, then you come alongside each buoy, then pull the thing on to the boat. A very delicate job.

Eilat town outside the kibbutz
The only hotel then was behind us, so we did not have too much trouble with curious tourists. They would just watch us for two weeks. We had parked near us an English couple. I used to bring them my English newspaper and they would make me a cup of tea in a very weird kettle that was hollow in the centre, where paper was put in and a fire was lit. Today, those two people are resident in Eilat. When they took off, they asked me what they could bring back, because they would come and live there. I said first of all they won't, but if they do come back, to bring me back a Rolls. Fay and Reg Morris laughed, and said they were coming back. Years later, I read in the paper that they did come back and that he was working in the hospital and was the director there. I was wrong about some people; they *did* come back to live there.

Eilat was a real exciting place. There were two hotels, very few staff, maybe four or five thousand inhabitants, and very few tourists were attracted – not like today. One of those enterprising con men brought whores for the Jordanian army in Aqaba.

Criminal policy: Army and Jacques' police experience

While I was there, the police in Tel Aviv decided that since Eilat was a new town, they were sending all the petty criminals down to re-educate them, instead of sending them to prison. It was a good idea, but they started to rob everybody in Eilat; but they never touched us, because we had nothing to steal, or probably, they thought we were the only honest guys in town. It got so bad that the police would lock up at night – it was like the Wild South. It really got out of hand in Aqaba. One trouble was when the British aircraft carrier came in – and the hoodlums brought hookers for the English soldiers, of course. Oh, yes, when I arrived I did not know that there were a lot of gangsters and juvenile delinquents that were sent from the North to try to help them. They had this little man in his fifties that had control over them, but it did not help. That is how bad things in the city were. They did not bother us on the kibbutz.

Then, one day, they brought in the army – and more police – and rounded up everybody that was there. How do I know this? I was one of the guys they arrested. A couple of weeks after being there, I was stopped by two soldiers and a policeman and was arrested. Apparently, they brought in a company of soldiers and picked up anybody that did not have an ID on him. I was just two feet from the gate. I yelled for someone, but no one came. It is always in life that when you are in trouble, no one comes. I saw Reg Morris and said, 'Will you tell these guys that I'm on that kibbutz?' He smiled and said all right, and went off. It didn't matter that the kibbutz was only 10 feet away. I protested by yelling to the people on the kibbutz, but nobody came out.

Eventually, someone did come, but it didn't help. We were taken to the City Hall, and there must have been hundreds – I met people there I knew, and one had his ID but didn't have his military card – and nobody came from the kibbutz to bail me out. Must have been there for hours, then someone came. I asked what took him so long; he said, 'We thought it was a joke!'

They took us to a big hall. There must have been hundreds and still more were brought in. After two hours, they started to process all of us. The army was there, checking that there were not deserters or criminals, etc. When it came to me, one of the policemen said, 'That one comes from the kibbutz.' So they phoned to see if it was true. Then they said, 'Why have you not got your papers?' I told them I was just a few feet away from the kibbutz when I was picked up. He gave me a piece of paper and said, 'I will summon you to court for not having your papers.' I was to go to court... one week later at 9.36 precisely.

Then, waiting there for me was Gilboa with a big smile and saying how was it. I said, 'You people took your time.' Two days later, the judge turned up to see what was there and if there was any case for the larger court; and if your case was minor, you just got a fine. I was in court with a lot of people – with the same problem. I always wondered: all the monies the court takes, where does it go to? One case was the man driving his motorbike and the girl behind was not sitting the right way. So, the judge asked why she was not sitting the right way, and the man replied, 'She refused to open her legs.' There was a roar of laughter, and the judge said 100 Israeli pounds. There was the company director that didn't have his driving licence. He tried to explain why, that he had it in his other trousers. The judge said that he should not talk any more or that would be five pounds. The director continued, and then bang, the judge... but you know how those company directors are: 10, 20, 30, 70, it was to 75 pounds before the director shut up. The judge had a sense of humour. One chap stood there, and he said to the accused, 'Why are you laughing?' He replied, so that cost another five pounds.

It was my turn and the accountant said, 'Don't you dare say anything at all. Remember, it is us paying; this not out of your pocket. Just plead guilty and that is all.' My name was called out, I went up to the judge and he read that on that day I did not have my ID on me, etc. Guilty or not? I said guilty, looking very serious. He looked at me, then back at his paper; five pounds. That was my first experience with the Jewish law. In going to court anywhere, you never win over the other side except for the judge and lawyers.

Momo's case
Even Momo had a touch with the law: he ran off and bit a boy. The father was not too happy, and we had to take Momo to the police station. On arriving there, on the desk of the sergeant, the first thing Momo did was to pee on the papers that lay there. The sergeant looked up and said, 'Out with him!' So, outside!

The police forces around the world are famous for the little gardens they have if there is space. So, he was tied up by a lead and then was tied to one of the gates so he would be able to walk around. Well, those few flowers there were eaten away, which did not make the policemen happy. They said, 'Take him back and prepare him to travel to Beersheba to get a check if he has any illness such as rabies.' So, we made him a box, put him in with food, and he was accompanied by a policeman. Everything went to plan; according to the policeman, when he arrived at the clinic, he went out for a minute, and on his return the doctor said Momo was okay, nothing wrong. Then we got a telegram saying that we must go there to put him back in his box. So, we phoned back, 'Why don't you give him a sleeping pill and that would be easy.' It is amazing that they could not think of something so easy. Then we paid a small fine. My, that monkey was becoming a very expensive luxury.

Eilot and democracy – reflections
One thing that always cannot be the same is when you get a sudden change, and I was preparing myself for leaving the place. Those that were coming seemed to me younger than me in experience, not in age. The atmosphere was changing and the characters that had gone away could not be replaced. Like the moving times, I look back at these people that were all searching for something new but were forced not to follow our ways.

Not too many people are able to arrive at the station and accept others' points of view. One thing is true: man and woman are great talkers. The question is, are we able to follow that road of equality? The answer is no; you will always have the disapproval of the majority – the minority is the failure to follow the misunderstanding of which side of the fence you are on. What do you accept as a way of life for yourself? Are you first, second, third and so on? Millions of books have been written with good intentions, but none are followed to the letter. Man has a built-in stop machine that refuses to let go of anything that is not to his pleasure. Whatever you may think of it, and all those do-gooders, one does not reach the top of the class by just knowledge, but by being in the right place at the right moment. All structures are the same. The thing is that one makes the wrong decision at times and keeps repeating it, cursing and saying, 'Why me?'

It is very rare that one can cope with more than one thought in our pretty little minds. More than this and you are confused and irrational. We go back to laziness; people call it progress, but it is wrong. It is not progress at all – it is a way to find how to live, dwell, without doing much movement. We were not made for sitting. It has got so bad that we humans have gone into jogging and running. That spare time could be used for more and better, which no one that I know of really does. I must admit, this made more sense than those old farts who give us all that idealistic bullshit.

Eilat retrospective

The last time I was in Eilat, they had moved the kibbutz out of the town, and the only people there were just one family from 1967... I learned a lot, though, about life on a kibbutz. The only thing that was bad: no money. So, if you want to go to a big city, you couldn't do much – we had a film a week, played concert – but what happens if you don't do those things? You are secured, or you were secured. They have changed; you can have a bank account and shoes! All ideals are good as long as you have people to follow them! Eilat was small, and everybody knew everybody that did crazy things. As for myself, I was young. The only thing I did that was wrong with the others was I would get drunk and chase the girls. I must admit Eilat wasn't boring; something was happening, day or night.

Jacques' War. 4th-10th June 1967: preparation, action, aftermath

Call-up

The Holy Land was where Sampson fought, and many others followed in his footsteps. I had just got back from my holiday in Europe when, overnight, the Middle East was boiling up again towards the gates of war. Nasser was yelling what he was going to do, and Levy Eshkol was doing the same.

Before I knew what was going on, I went straight to my headquarters and was sent down near Kibbutz Gvulot, which was the second line of information. Here we had the 35-year-olds and upward. There were only maybe 20 or 25 youngsters. We started digging in, making our defence with the highest effort. The area we were placed in was right on top of a rubbish dump. Don't laugh – it really smelled. Digging the mixes of sand and rubbish isn't funny. We must have been four companies away with the digging. As always, when it came to digging, I did my best to break the shovel, as by the time everybody had finished the trench, we all had to return to camp. Alas, this time wasn't, as we dug and dug. In between we had lunch – and it wasn't fun; the smell was just awful.

Everybody thought that we would be at war. Nasser had already kicked out the UN from the Sinai and the Gaza Strip, and we kept digging. After a couple of days, the rubbish began to take shape. It looked quite a defence spot. I doubt very much if we could have stopped any well-equipped force, though every night the tank column would retreat to their night position. The noise they made was like an earthquake from a mile away; it shook the ground, making you feel like it was the end of the world – but we got our kick out of it. One night, one of the tanks hit off the track and went on a mine, which only damaged its chain.

The nights were cold and windy, and I was very ill-equipped. I had no sleeping bag except for a couple of blankets. I was then up most of the night because I was chattering my teeth off, and it woke all the other soldiers around me. I succeeded in getting a pair of socks because when I arrived here, I didn't even have my shaving kit, and I was in sandals and socks. You'd think that they would have supplies, which they didn't have at all. There were only two guys that did have anything to wear; one, from Rehovot, was a scientist. The mood at the start was quite cheerful, but slowly things became tense. When you think it's your last day on earth, you just don't want to sit around doing nothing. So, we started to play games of poker as a distraction, and we then had a singsong.

As I passed the Radio 8 communication, the control said to me, 'One more note and we will still be at war.'

I smiled and went back to tell the guys. They didn't take it too lightly. I said the only time Israel will attack is when Nasser blocks the Gulf of Aqaba. Then, for sure, we will be at war with no way out, since we cannot go through the Suez Canal. We were not yet comfortable enough. One soldier said we should start planting trees so we could have some shade. I think he must have been a farmer.

I finally realised we might be stuck here for quite a while. Someone was sending me letters and parcels and I was wondering if I'd ever see anybody anymore. We were all given a paper to sign in case something happened, like an assurance. I left everything to my aunt. After a week of walking about without a weapon, it was fun, as I did not have to clean it. I felt like a real tramp.

Four hours a day we drilled. It's a common thing in the army, always keep the troops busy; if not, they go crazy. It was fun watching the old

CHAPTER 8: JACQUES' WRITINGS: ISRAEL, 1956-1972

guys storming into a building. The most important thing for any soldier anywhere is self-survival, even in a gang; always remember your self-survival course. Unless you storm an objective, then you're out in the open, then it's the bullet or foot mine that gets you. I doubt very much today if I would be able to run like I did 10 years ago, but on the other hand it would surprise you that a guy of 50 would do just as good a job when it's necessary.

So, in 1967 Jacques would have been 29.

In the evening, they had a show. I was so tired that day that I made a miss and went to sleep. As far as the political arena, there was no news. On Saturday, we had a game and the company that won would get a 24-hour leave. Of course, we won – we had to run through a set of obstacles, over ladders, a swimming pool, etc.

Somebody even wanted my 24-hour pass. No chance! I had to get away from this place; it really was getting me down. Yes, the war was around the corner and all I wanted was my bed. When I got home, I went straight to bed and slept for 10 hours without a stop.

War: preparation
When I got up, while having my coffee, I heard on the radio that Nasser had blocked the Gulf of Aqaba. I knew for sure that it wouldn't be long before the war would start. When anybody is cornered, they fight back with any means available. My 24-hour pass was at its end. I rushed back to our meeting point. Believe it or not, they were on time for once. I got into the bar, saying hello to the guys like I have known them for the last 20 years, as in 10 days, in a very close environment, you get to know them very well. Every single thing in your character is stripped down; they even know which side you sleep best. We surely needed this holiday for what it was worth for me: it was sleep. I doubt very much that if I met any of

157

the company today, they would remember me or anybody else. Those were two rotten weeks.

As we drove along the windy road, we came upon a blockade with Military Police telling us that the 54th Battalion had been posted from Gevulat to Gaza. Ho! Ho! Here we go again. I said to myself all my stuff was in Gevulat, and I was still wearing my sandals, but I had brought a sleeping bag with me. As we arrived at another settlement, we saw the camp. Everybody didn't look so happy; what was going on was defensive, now we were in the attacking line in a sense.

> They were in a kibbutz near Gaza, but I don't know which one. Nir Yitzak,(8 hostages and 5 dead in 2023 Hamas attack) and Gvulot are possibilities. 2023),and Gvulot are possible. 100 people killed there October 2023.

Supposed strategy
All we were supposed to do really was to mop up after the spearhead had broken through; we would position our face at the strategic joint and hold it. We were now equipped with quite heavy machine guns and four bazookas neatly packed so when we got there they would be dismantled and ready for use. The night was here, and as we listened for the news, it really didn't sound good to all of us. Someone that had come back from their 24-hour pass had brought some goodies like sausages, cake, etc. We laid everything out like having our last meal, for tomorrow was going to be a big day – big night day.

- Whoever thought I would be caught in such a mess? Another war in my book, but I was still an idealist in my own ways, not fanatical but an idealist.

We were all in the kibbutz main room and we went to sleep there. I got up at my usual hour, six o'clock, washed, then walked about the kibbutz, seeing its members going to their daily work. I wish I could join them. I was really in a mood for anything else – as I thought, true ßor false?

The army cook was a young guy so, as could well be expected, it was just the regular meal. The only time I tasted good food in the army was when we were doing border patrol, and we had a cook from one of the best hotels in town. With the rubbish they gave us, he made it look like something off a French kitchen.

War breaks out

Soon, everybody was awake, and I took off to the toilet. As I squatted, I suddenly found someone yelling that the war had broken out, then a rumbling started off in all places. I wanted to take it easy like a good British general but rushed out. Someone showed me and must have said to himself what a funny place to be at a time like this. From eight a.m. the bombs were falling all over the place. All you could do was just sit there and listen for Cairo Radio saying that they had already passed Gaza – and that Umm Kulthum (the iconic Egyptian singer) would finish her song in Tel Aviv.

I managed to get the BBC, as usual; they were talking about the possibility that if Israel overran Sinai, it would keep it this time, etc. Still the bombs were falling, and it was midday. We were issued c-rations, which isn't much: most of it is dry, so it makes you want to drink like an elephant. Although most of the men had lost their appetite, there's always someone that will eat double. Indeed, there was someone that sat there and went through a ration that was enough for five people.

Then they got us to move. We got into our command car, then shot off in the direction of Nahal Oz, which faces Gaza. All those famous hills of El Moutar and El Cuber (*I cannot find on map*) where Israel lost many good soldiers in 1956 and Turkey lost 10,000 men in the First World War. The hill can't even be called a hill – there isn't much of a climb, but you do sit on top of your enemy. When you're there like this, you couldn't get a hernia from running. I was glad that we didn't have to storm it; the regulars would do this running through minefields while being fired upon – what is called a diversion to mix up the enemy by thinking that it's the main force attacking, while at the side the spearhead would make its way through, eliminating military tactic. I'm positive that the general facing us knew this! Modern war hasn't changed much more than the weapon of destruction. These days the casualties are higher, as even the soldiers will always be used to storm any objective.

We were outnumbered three to one – their entrenchment was based on the Russian defence, which, of course, are very well defended to the hilt. On each side of them they had tanks intended to support heavy machine guns. This is the usual way, with heavy mortars in the back of them to pin anything down that approached them with the firepower of the devil.

On that day, it was quite warm and the shade of the trees on the road to Gaza kept us cooled down. Bombs were still falling in mild doses, but the settlement a mile away was getting shelled. The shelling had already damaged the kibbutz good and proper, and many of its animals were killed; and you can be sure that the chickens that day didn't lay any eggs.

News came in saying that the Air Force had wiped out over 200 planes, but nobody believed it. We never saw one plane about, so our conclusion was it was just propaganda. Then a bus full of journalists went past. They looked like they didn't fit the occasion. Five minutes later, the bus was making a fast retreat, and they looked very pale indeed. Later on, I heard that they were told that Gaza was taken, which was a fault, of course.

The afternoon was passing away when the Chief Rabbi of the armed forces turned up, giving every soldier a piece of paper with the Shema before going to battle, saying as he went past, 'To kill them till the last sperm.' Coming from a religious man, I was really amazed; it sounded like a medieval war. As he gave me one, I crossed myself the Christian way and he smiled and walked on.

Twenty minutes later, we were given the order to move. That meant that the spearhead must have broken through; but as the situation was still in action with the bombardment getting worse than ever, what the hell was going on? Then word came that the decoy company was completely pinned down with very high casualties – and that the spearhead had been ambushed 10 miles off Gaza, and was still engaged in a full-scale battle.

Attack, ill-prepared
We were ordered to attack, believe it or not, but we were not very equipped to attack anybody. Come to think of it, the diversion wasn't good, either. Like I have said, they were supposed to knock at the front door and the spearhead was to overrun the two positions. So, on that bright afternoon, the enemy occupying both spots were waiting at full strength. Oh, yes, they also had the sun at the back of them, which made visibility hard for us – as off we went in the direction of the blinding sun with five ill-equipped command cars which didn't have anything to do with this kind of battle. What we really needed was armour, or at least more of everything. We dashed off around the left side of the settlement, then headed off straight at them. Some of the members of the settlement waved to us to come into their bunker, and I wish I could have done this. Out of this confusion, everybody thought that the battle was over and the only thing that was happening was the mopping-up.

We didn't get 500 yards from the settlement when the bombardment started more furious than before, and it was really concentrated in a small area, and vision was so bad. The explosion, which we could not hear, produced dust and a battery there was spotted and was very efficient. It got us pinned down for four hours. We couldn't move – just lay flat on the ground. Even if we had a shovel, the chance of digging ourselves in would have been quite impossible. Yes, as I said, from the confusion communication was dead. No one knew what was happening at the front and the Chief Rabbi of the armed forces was with us. His only weapon was the Torah and his shofar as we drove towards the enemy; he was blowing it. It sounds ridiculous, but it's true as I'm writing it at this moment.

I was scared out of my wits for about four or five seconds, then I just didn't care. As I looked about, everybody looked pale, including me; probably death was staring us in the face, although it was a peak summer day. I don't really remember feeling the heat of the day; lying down, one can only crawl about and wonder whether you will come out alive in one piece. One keeps yelling for everybody, if anybody is hit, and if the person doesn't answer, you crawl up. If he is shocked, you just slap him. There was quite a lot of slapping in four and a half hours. A high percentage of the casualties is made by the shelling when storming a defence area. First, you get shells upon them; if you're still in good condition and get through, then you run through fields of landmines in addition to this machine gun fire, rifle fire – anything that can shoot is fired at you.

The objective was in a mess of messes. A hundred yards from the enemy entrapment was a company with 75% of its force wiped out; the others couldn't retreat because of being shot or bombarded – and our five command cars were pinned down and the rest of the company column that was supposed to follow us got lost and went straight into the mouth of the lion. All this happened less than 20 minutes after their departure. One truck was loaded with bedding and the kitchen, and a couple of trucks with heavy machine guns that were supposed to be erected for defence purposes once we entered Gaza. This we nearly dismantled and tightened up neatly as the only defence we had was small arms.

What a balls up, and the whole operation was supposed to take two hours. In actual fact, it took 25 hours before it ended. Every inch of the city of Gaza was under siege – it's not a beautiful sight, scared people not knowing what awaits them – but still the battle raged. They fought bravely, and so did we. We moved many wounded out of the area back to safety, where a field hospital was erected.

At nightfall
After dark, we started to move up to the boundary of this very well-fortified hill, with defences double fenced with landmines and empty

food cans on the fences so when disturbed, they rattled, and the enemy would probably open fire with everything they had at the area the noise came from. Like I have described to the best of my ability, fortification is an area where every weapon is placed so one covers the other. I shall draw a picture on the next page like a symphony, with all the instruments playing their part in a full-scale battle. Not even a cat would dare to face it or crawl through it – man must be mad to do it.

I wasn't, yet we still produced weapons of mass destruction so complicated that we have come to the point now that we can eliminate hundreds of millions of people in seconds without being there. This is done because we need to be secure and safe as long country has the weapon that can tear the heart of any country in less time than before.

Battle
Just before we took off to battle, there was an announcement that said Jordan had declared war on Israel. Ninety percent of our company were given their age of 35+; not any good to anybody in military style. Yet they produced wonders. Most of them were overweight, far out of being even fit for anything but washing dishes or office work. We took off into the unknown. The sky was starting to overcloud, and the bombardment made visibility hard. We were facing Gaza with the sun at our back, and the enemy had everything going for them: they had ambushed the spearhead, they had destroyed the diversion that was now covering itself among the ruins of its armour, which was completely out of action, and we were pinned down in a cotton field as the bombs kept coming down like a thunderstorm, the shrapnel whizzing past us, sometimes hitting the stems, making the whole cotton plant fall down like a tree.

There was no fear left in me; I was relaxing away. All I could think while I was lying there was how good it would be if I was in bed reading a good book. We got the Chief Rabbi back in the line with his torah and his shofar. I find it quite stupid that he had to come with us in the first place. A man of God is supposed to help, but should never aid or say anything about destruction, though today many have their doubts if such a god exists at all.

Morning
The sun was slowly dropping behind the hill. I could see now where the diversion was destroyed. I must admit, I don't know why they didn't attack us; we were completely pinned down. With the force they had, they could have taken over the settlement. They had the firepower, including the manpower. One thing about bombardment is that when you're in it, you don't hear them land; you can hear them being fired, but as for falling on you, you don't hear them, but when you do, it means that you're safe. Their battery commander was very well trained; he was directing the fire like a darts champion. After the battle, many searched for him, and some of us wanted to knock his block off (*not Jacques*). Fortunately, he wasn't found, which I think was just as well, because I deeply disapproved – but he was a great spotter in my book, due to the fact that the enemy didn't have to fight for its existence or conquer at a speed like the Israelis, to their disadvantage in a way. Their forces were moveable, they could have easily pushed us back quite a few miles without resistance whatsoever, but in battle many ways changed. That commander didn't use the same fact of being drawn into an ambush and the bombardment was easing, since darkness was approaching; like this we would only be shot at more.

Later – afternoon
Later on, in the whole area the dark sky was a very dark red, like we were trying very much to change the darkness back into daylight, as much of a beating was going on that I doubt very much if anybody took any notice of it. They were well-equipped; flares were sent up every minute to keep the area alight so as to stop us advancing. As I kept thinking of that soft bed, I could put in 24 hours of sleep without any trouble whatsoever. Keeping moving from being wounded and still sane hopefully… since the communication was broken, we had to return a runner, which took a long time finding out the grave situation we were in at that very moment. We finally started to pull back and make a detour on very hollow ground

so the bullets would be body height. So, our movement would be more relaxed and faster to the enemy position. In the Israeli army there isn't such a thing as a retreat, but to go back and regroup and attack again and again. We went to the front door to knock, and the door was slammed in our faces – they really had the firepower.

We stormed the hills six times without success. They had a villain well positioned in a cement pillar box, firing freely without any problem whatsoever. The major and four soldiers that were about 200 yards from them got up to them with a bazooka and continued in the battle. We caught up with them, noticing that it was the only heavy piece they had on that side. We spread in a chain while still under fire from light weapons like rifles, machine guns, grenades, etc.

We started to advance, not realising that we were going through a minefield. What I really mean is that we forgot about the minefield. Shit! Was that something, as we advanced towards the enemy position? The guy on my right went up on a mine at the same time as the guy on my left. You can really imagine what went through my mind, like: suppose I lay down and pretend I'm wounded or dead, or even fainted – anything just to get out alive. The time of night I don't really remember much. We finally reached their trench and eliminated each of them. They fought bravely, and we even had face-to-face combat, which is very rare these days. My second caught a bullet that grazed his cheek and he was shot at the end of his ear. He gave a yell, then sat down. I didn't wait to see if he was alive or dead – it's one thing one doesn't do: stop in the middle of an attack, especially like the foul-up that was going on. Out of many 500 or 600 men, maybe 80% of them were casualties at the end of the battle; maybe there must be maybe 15 or 16 that came out without a scratch. Sorry, just remembered, 17 soldiers came out of El Cubah without a scratch.

> *The best account of the Gaza attack I found is here. Apparently, they were surrounding Khan Yunis and Sheikh Zuweid, to get control routes to El Arish and El Quantara via the Rafah gap. I cannot identify place names in Jacques' memoir on map.*

We then made a stop, then the spearhead finally got us young, healthy para troops that had already fought their way out of an ambush. Anyway, we were still on our way to the heart of their concrete defence – during the wait of battle on the hill, we saw the farmers still working their crop, as we thought that bombarding them was pointless at the time. Later, I heard that a farmer was really a soldier dressed up as a farmer and was really planting mines from right to left and centre, so that even a cat would have problems going through. The game of war is very important for any country, and the most dangerous enemy one can have is a country that has no minerals or cannot support itself. When they go to war, there is nothing to lose but man himself. He can gamble away – as for a country that is self-sufficient, its difference is that it will lose more if it loses. At the time, my thoughts were far from understanding these problems. Call me naïve, but it didn't come into my mind; it was just a game – an experience that I wanted to go through. In a way, I still want to experience things that I have missed, through someone out of my reach. The bombardment was slowly dying down and we could still hear small arms fire at a distance. We held our ground; those that were not wounded seriously walked about, checking as though one was in a department store. The smell in the air was strong of bodies torn up by cannon fire, and probably tanks that went over bodies while in the attack.

Wounded

I didn't see the final defeat of the second hill (*El Le Mocta Hora?*). Whether it was one of our guys that threw a hand grenade or not I don't know, for at the time I was already hiding from a shell that fell near my back and part of my left shoulder. I was a real bloody sight; the grenade exploded, and the shrapnel lodged itself in my wrist, disconnecting a vital link to my hand. Literally, they had to yank out the weapon I was holding still in my left hand. When I was taken to the field hospital, it looked like there were hundreds of men laid on stretchers.

The doctor there took a look at me as though I was supposed to lay down and die. I was stripped down to my underwear. Nearby, they were operating on an emergency. Then the doctor said, 'You are cleared; you have only one technical wound.'

Then, to finish the treatment, one of the drivers that was bringing the casualties from the battlefield back and forth, headed straight towards a tree. He crashed into it; apparently, the soil must have been slippery. The tree didn't let the truck go forward and the engine was still running, and so were the wheels on the spot. The doctor that was taking care of me rushed off to the truck and yelled at the driver, thinking that he had been shot. He noticed that the driver was in a state of shock, so he jumped over the driver and switched off the engine, then gave the driver a good slap across the face. The driver yelled, 'What happened? What happened? How the hell did I get here?' It's amazing how one's brain can go blank and not remember what one does. The doctor brought him back, asking one of the male nurses if he knew how to drive. At that moment, the original driver said, 'You can't do that! I signed for the truck!' And he dashed off back to the battlefield.

I think the doctor forgot me. My wound was starting to be painful. 'Hey, doctor, you haven't finished with me,' I said. He came with a smile, noticed that I was in pain, and took out a small tube and unscrewed the end, which had a needle. He injected it and within a few minutes I was in the mood for laughing myself sick! Though I kept a serious face, I couldn't believe with all the wounded and dead there I could laugh. I got up and the male nurse said, 'Don't get up; it will be much better for you to sit down.' But I just couldn't. I realised maybe they were the guys of the company. I couldn't believe that I was the only one that survived. I must say, there were a couple of thousand, but I couldn't believe that none of them made it to the field hospital.

Maverick: A memoir of Jacques Kornbrot, 1938 - 2014

Ambulances were coming back from the hospital, and we were loaded on them. On one stretcher was the company sergeant major, out cold. I don't know whether he was breathing, but that was one person I knew. Then the convoy of ambulances headed towards Ashkelon Hospital. On the way, the ambulance ahead of us was fired upon by a group of the enemy that worked their way into the road. Even with all the wounded, the ambulance driver ended up being himself driven to hospital on a stretcher.

On arriving at hospital, since I was still able to walk around, I went from one ward to another, seeing if I knew anybody there. Someone was waving his hand, but he was unrecognisable; he received a full dose of shrapnel in his face, which produced complete thinning of the blood. He looked like a wolf. He started to talk, and it was Shaul. I then turned to the nurse without thinking and asked her if he was going to live! She didn't even have time to answer. He yelled at me, 'Of course I'm going to live!' I never felt so like an idiot. I was then taken to a bus that was converted into an ambulance mobile with about 15 or 20 stretchers. I passed out as I laid down. The last time I had a decent sleep was about two weeks ago. That injection was really potent. I woke up later laid on a table completely naked, with a doctor examining my whole body. It's not something I would wish anybody when waking up. He commented that I was all right from the outside, then I was rushed off to a hall and put into bed in a white sheet. The bed was hard – it felt like I was back in the trenches. I wasn't even dozing off when the stretcher came. I was put on it – damn, what next? I was being X-rayed – no comment.

Morning in the hospital
The morning was here. The thing that I hate about hospitals is that they start your day with checking if you've got a fever. I must admit that the one thing I don't have is the ability of getting a fever like other people. I remember when we were doing border patrol, we had a lot on our hands as we laid about making bets who had the highest fever – I always had the lowest; maybe it's good, maybe it's bad, I don't know. Then we

had breakfast, cleaned up again, and the doctor came by telling us that everybody was healthy. Even the guy next to me had a bullet implanted in one of his testicles and he would be operated on. On the other side of me was a chap that received a blow on the head, and he was still unconscious. I got up, but the nurses always like to see their patients in bed – it was war again. I politely told her that I could walk, but this didn't help – she just said, 'Back to bed!' So I waited until she went off and I got up and went into the sunshine...

Nature of wounding
It's amazing what way and how one gets wounded, like a sabre cut. There was the soldier whose helmet stopped a bullet going into his head. The bullet was half in the helmet and then went into the soldier less than a half inch – he kept walking around, showing his lucky escape. Then another bullet went from one of his behind to the other, making five holes coming out, but no serious damage.

To pass the time, I went from one room to another, asking what story they had for me. I think the best one was a soldier that went home with his submachine gun – and showed it to his family, forgot to take the magazine out and shot dead his mother, wife, and wounded his children. He was in complete shock. The police were checking his story and all he wanted to do was show how the submachine gun worked. To some he was a cook or just a storekeeper; a pro wouldn't have got himself in such a mess, though accidents like that happen in the field in the camp.

Advising a young soldier
Then, as I was lying back on my bed for a break, in front of me appeared this very young Moroccan lad that, to this day, I wonder how the hell he ever got into a company where they could easily be his father or grandfather. One of his problems was that he didn't know any Hebrew, just French and probably Arabic. He spoke to me, and I suppose he probably got wounded in the bombardment, because I didn't see him after the attack to the hills. He sat down and said that he got as far as the cotton fields, where

the bombardment got out of hand. He intended to lay down and receive the bombardment, he said. 'I just threw my weapon away in retreat. In my running, I was wounded in the arm.' I told him that he shouldn't repeat that to anybody or else the army could give punishment, though he looked like a hero. He felt that he had done the right thing. What can you expect from a very young soldier lost in this war that probably didn't mean anything to him? He wanted to live.

Jacques was for life and fought senseless deaths.

State of war and return to unit
News came in that they were still trying very hard to get to the top of the Golan Heights. The Israelis had to open up a road to get to the top. The loss of manpower was high; one can equal it to the Monte Cassino episode. Everyone in the room kept saying why don't they sneak through? – as though we thought it was a piece of cake. I made friends with a guy that was on the diversion: the company that was knocked out within 10 minutes of arrival. We decided to return to our unit because it was crazy lying about doing nothing but waiting to get our quarterly injection. We asked the doctor if he could give us a note of how much more injections we needed and we would return to the field and get them there. He agreed, and we took to Tel Aviv first. The place didn't look like there was a war on like in 1956. There was still a lot of people moving about as though there wasn't a war at all. The first thing we did was to buy a Mifal Hapach, a lottery ticket for what it was worth. Then he invited me to have dinner on the bus restaurant, which only members eat there. He belonged to a group company of the buses that does the whole of Tel Aviv. Anyone that belongs with them is quite well off. Since nightfall was coming again like a disease, we decided we would go back tomorrow morning and he took off in one direction and I went in mine.

Visiting aunt in Tel Aviv, then kibbutz
I took off to see my aunt, spent the usual 10 minutes with her and then took off to Kibbutz Negba, since it would make me be closer to Gaza.

Samson had a pain there, so did I. In 1948, Negba was the front line; but its buildings were completely knocked down, except for the tower, which is still standing to this day. As I arrived there, the sun had already disappeared. Because of the war, one had to be sure you would not show light. I went straight to the dining room and was greeted happily indeed. I told them I had just come out of hospital, and I was on my way back to my outfit that was in Gaza.

Kuba and Rachel came up to me and took me to their room, I mean house, and I stayed the night. The next day, I got up early and we went to the dining room for breakfast. From the sight of all the young girls, like me, they were all in the army and were all probably fighting on the Golan Heights. The kibbutz was in a sense deserted, like Tel Aviv was in 1956. The elders were running the kibbutz again. Most of all, the heavy work that was usually done by the young was postponed. Most of the older members don't retire to live in the city. They do, of course, work less hours – four to five hours a day – and today we find out that retirement has had, after a lifetime of forced labour, you are addicted to work to fulfil the 24 hours you live in. Before technology arrived, we were much healthier than we are today; all our systems worked. Days go by on the kibbutz when things can get very boring. I guess we can't win in the end. But we do our best to make people think there is change, and life will be better. The achievement, as it's called, can be misleading when you get to middle-age. Seeing the matter really was that it's like a well-cooked meal: it leaves you with the thought there shall be a better meal to come.

Getting back to unit and UN units

I got out to the main road and caught a bus that brought me to the outskirts of Ashkelon; from there I hitch-hiked the rest of the way to Gaza. First, as we were about to enter, was a whole contingent of UN troops from India. Apparently, some of them didn't make it out of the Strip to safe ground and probably were in Gaza during the war. A small group was stuck in a pocket of the battlefield and was eliminated. When we finally took their position, I thought at that moment that we were fighting the whole world now. As we passed them, most of the soldiers yelled at them, 'You bastards!', etc., all in English, of course.

The incident for which Jacques got a medal. Willy Halpert has details I cannot publish. Jacques himself never told me.

Greeted by comrades

Since the wounds of war were still fresh as I walked into headquarters, there was a ring of shouts and lots of movement. The major was telling off two soldiers who were caught playing poker with the enemy, not more than 10 hours before we were killing each other. These two soldiers already had a game of poker going; what a riot. Anybody that knew how to drive, drove. The first couple of days was like the Wild West on the roads of Gaza. I then went to my outfit and, to my surprise, it wasn't as bad as I had thought. Most of my section was still alive and well. Interesting really, when there is no law on the road or street. First accident rarely happened, even when driving four or five [at least]. It wasn't until the military police took over that accidents occurred. Just like this, everything was normal. In fact – I wouldn't be surprised that if there was no policing, the world might be a little better. You would still have those that dominated the rest as always, but crime might be even better controlled in a way.

Atmosphere as war ended

The atmosphere was still very tense. The conflict was on, and the odd civilian old man was moving across the square, not even taking any notice that we were there. I would not be surprised if he was here during the First World War. An Israeli soldier walked over and yelled at him; he turned around with a smile – what could you really do to this old man? The soldier was probably baffled and walked him to where he was going. Most of the soldiers are not the ones who fight in battle, but those that are in back to take over their position. They sound like the hero that never was, yelling at the prisoners. All the soldier that didn't want to go to battle stayed behind, refusing at the time to follow commands. There were quite a few.

After the battle, they acted like they did something the colonel didn't want to even be bothered with at all. All they could do was look about for loot, for they didn't have the shadow of the battle on their mind. We sent them to the headquarters to do guarding, plus the kitchen toilet. If I was in that situation, I wouldn't have turned up at all; I would have hidden or made myself sick from bottom to top. Why these people turn up to not wanting to fight in the first place it's beyond my understanding – making an idiot of themselves before other human beings, but day by day you have them all around, looking for sympathy – and I know many of them. The self-pity I imagine these poor souls put in front of themselves was: I don't care about anything but myself; and they gave something, and it was like the end of the world. When one compares this war with other wars, it was quick. Telling us it was the kind of war that in the future shall be done by the same method by speed of light; but if one slowed down the time would come that you would have to dig in like the old days of the trenches.

CHAPTER 9.
REFLECTIONS AND LEGACY

Overview

There are three sections: Jacques' childhood reflections, Jacques' adult reflections, Jacques' reflections on achievement, and my summary. Jacques' reflections are diffuse and repetitive, but I have erred on the side of over-inclusion, as I want people to receive Jacques' own words as much as possible. Jacques' reflections come from deeply emotional personal experience, but, of course, he was well aware that neither the problems nor the solutions he suggests are new. We start form endpoint: his ashes scattered in 2015 by the farm he loved.

2015 Villeherviers. Top: wood where some of Jacques' ashes are buried. Bottom: farm

Childhood reflections

Jacques reflects on his personal childhood in the, perhaps forlorn, hope that his experiences will influence positive change. The first theme is motherhood and what can go wrong. The next theme is parenting, with emphasis on the need for commitment and sacrifice for 18 years, and the reasons people do, nevertheless, become parents. Education is another area where Jacques was royally failed by the system, as he describes. He then reflects on how society intervenes when things go wrong, including fostering that may be better than birth parenting.

What is unchanged since 1938-1956 in France, Australia, UK
- The best interests of the child supposedly come first.
- By default, the birth family is the best environment to raise children. Furthermore, neither birth nor foster parents require training. Good parenting is believed to be 'instinctive'.
- Attempts are made to remedy poor birth family environments before fostering.
- Foster care is usually superior to institution care. The media has many examples of abusive and exploitative institutions. Hence resources are focussed on fostering.

What has changed since 1938-1956 in the UK?
- There is greater emphasis on keeping contact between the foster and birth family, where possible; but locating foster parents near birth parents may be difficult.
- There is training for foster parents and for families of problem children (ADHD, autism, etc., now known as 'neuro-diverse'), but still none for birth parents of normal children ('neuro-typical').
- Children are told early when they are fostered. It came as a complete shock to Jacques.
- During fostering, efforts are made to create and maintain contact with birth parents. Geography may be a serious problem (for Jacques during the Second World War it was impossible).

CHAPTER 9: JACQUES' REFLECTIONS: PARENTING, CHILDHOOD, SOCIAL STRUCTURE

- After a return to the birth parent(s), efforts are made to maintain contact with foster families. This was actively discouraged in earlier times: Jacques did not even know the town of his foster parents.
- Social services in the UK usually remain responsible for the welfare of children taken into their care until age 18, even after a return to the birth parents. This implies monitoring, and hence resources.
- Children are entitled to be consulted about their care, but age is vague.
- Children, birth, and foster parents are all entitled to separate representation.

Adult reflections

Jacques' reflections are informed by experiences on kibbutzim, the army and wide travel. He views humans as lazy and motivated by desire for comfort, respect, and control of their own lives. Obviously, these motivations may lead to war and violence, but Jacques does not seem to have any notion of violence or sadism for its own sake. He reflects on desires to build a better world (kibbutz movement, emigrants to USA, Israel) and failure due to inbuilt copying of previous generations, and failure of institutions at every level. He ends up bitter and disillusioned with France, Australia, Israel, UK, and wants only to be alone. He was generous to individuals but refused to vote or join or support any organisation, large or small. Nevertheless, he felt, but resisted, a compulsion to return and fight for Israel in the 1974 Yom Kippur War. He had been an idealist but felt his various countries had betrayed him and somehow failed to let him contribute to the better world we had all hoped for. He reflects on progress through life and the nature of achievements.

Maverick: A memoir of Jacques Kornbrot, 1938 - 2014

Jacques' childhood reflections

Motherhood: an example of poor mothering, his mother

Oh, yes, that woman mother that was forced on me, how she tried for me to be affectionate to her. In that flat I had to sleep in the same bed with her night after night. I wasn't free anymore. I was a prisoner from age seven. When I did something wrong, she wouldn't hit me, but would put her fingernail right into my flesh and it would look like I had been scratched by a cat or a chicken, and, in the process, I got those marks. I don't really know what my cousin thought of that; probably stayed neutral.

> *People did not defend Jacques' interests if it meant confronting his mother's comfort. One of many examples of prioritising the birth parent.*

This woman had a lot of ups and downs in her daily life – one minute she was happy, the second depressed, with a stream of hate and the foul language to go with it. I just didn't understand. She tried very hard to be a mother in many ways, but she wasn't made to be a mother. She didn't know the involvement or the time it takes, the sacrifices one person has to make, yet suffering. She came from a very large family and was educated well enough with all the foundations, yet she didn't know how to give love that I mostly needed. I was a burden. Her life wasn't as she expected the harvest of sowing the seeds. Yet people have judged me as in the wrong. A crime was committed, but not by me, and I can apologise to no one. That's life, is all one can say. This woman should never have become a mother in the first place. She was incapable mentally of dealing with her problems. She should have stayed single or married without having any children at all. But who am I to judge?

> *Even in his misery, Jacques has some insight, and even sympathy, for his mother's situation.*

CHAPTER 9: JACQUES' REFLECTIONS: PARENTING, CHILDHOOD, SOCIAL STRUCTURE

Yes, my mother always succeeded in getting everyone on her side; a real laugh. No one ever thought to tell her to wise up and be realistic. Yet there are millions of people like her, and, believe me, I keep away from them. I won't put up with the agony and frustration anymore. That is, everyone thought it more important to keep peace round the family. My mother could only think of herself. Even her letters that were written long before I was born are of a complainer.

Parenting

What is a happy childhood?
But let me go back to when I was a happy child with no worries or cares. It was a good, pleasant life, but with no night light except for candles. It was a very quiet Farm, except for the animals and those who would pass by on the road in a buggy.

My foster parents, who at the time I truly thought were my parents, cared about me like they should. Although, my Papa in the corner of his eyes at times would've liked to beat the hell out of me. Yet he remained strong and kept his hand to himself. I don't remember at all anybody hitting me or yelling.

> *Jacques describes a good environment in which to grow up and develop, mentally, physically, and morally. He emphasises that a child needs to be loved and cared for. There was no physical punishment, or even shouting on the Farm. The worst that could happen was 'Papa did not give me one of his big smiles today'. He observed a good example of someone tempted to hit out who controlled himself. It made a lifelong impression.*

Society's view of parenthood
Society can't change the stream of laws which are laid down from generation to generation. This pure laziness of us all and failure to take

responsibility are statues frozen in ice. When we look at the way nations fight each other and bring upon us the cruelty of war – and its aftermath. For those few enjoyable moments that you are in bed with a girl, how can you produce a baby you don't really think of for the next 18 or so years?

This compulsion of an adult towards a child is to follow the law of some sect. But no one can tell you the truth because it is hurtful to hear or understand. Spending more time giving is rare and it is a crime towards nature. If it's done, it's always the baddies that rule us, because we can always forgive or blame them for their actions if things don't turn out right. The laws are never followed, though. They are broken and reinstated to the case of the party as quickly done. We, the grown-ups, what have we to look forward to following our parents' footsteps, building our house bigger?

Yes, it should never have happened. The bringing up of a child to the world is more than just going to bed. No one looks at the problem or is educated in that field. Unfortunately, all we turn up with is saying how terrible it is. Whoa, life itself is like the art with its paintings; way ahead it goes up – and then we are educated.

There was a period that was very advanced for its time. Then it falls back a thousand years, yet the body is the same and the mind is the same. From these beautiful creative designs, we overlook too many items, like why should we start at this point? It's quite simple really when you come down to it. You have the Bible, which has quite a good set of laws, and then you can even try Dr Spock that sold millions – and after 20 years admit that he made a mistake on how to bring up a child.

> *Optimum child-rearing practices remain controversial among experts and lay folk alike! Jacques and I remain sceptics about ;experts'.*

CHAPTER 9: JACQUES' REFLECTIONS: PARENTING, CHILDHOOD, SOCIAL STRUCTURE

Reasons for parenthood and role of parents
There are many people today who commit the biggest crime by having children and not taking care of them, not knowing the first thing about it. To be a parent, you must give so much love and patience with understanding. It is hard to go through these early years without a problem. One must set a book of rules and follow it to the bitter end. With my mother, she started and never finished. She made the rules as she went along, and they were all contradictory. It's rare that parents give all they've got. They don't want to feel cheated; it sounds like a business deal that goes on.

Yet, in the long term, if you go through the hardship of a child and come out with a normal brain, you have achieved one thing: to stay sane. These criminal parents of wonder dream of luck and don't really fail in their life, for they have their children to blame for this. It's always the child's fault for their downfall.

Blame the victim.

There are not too many happy people today who can say their childhood was a happy one. Even on normal grounds, the complaints have been heard for many hundreds of years and will continue as long as one doesn't have the patience to sit down and arrange steps to the following of man and woman if it's right for them to love children or not.

Many can't wait to have a home out of their parents' way and get married with no idea what they're getting themselves into socially and economically. A plant can always be uprooted and replanted, but human beings are not able to do that. They might change their name, religion, even nationality or, political view, but down deep in our programmed mind we stay the same! In those groups of following the leader – or being followed – or changing as it pleases the person. As far as I can remember, after being taken from my foster parents, to the best of my knowledge, I stayed the same.

Responsibilities of parents

When the child is practically minded, then no way are you going to convince him by just words alone. Once that little baby came out of the mother's womb, boy, you have one of the greatest responsibilities falling on you. You have to give attention to them. More than that, you have to accept the honest truth to bring them up. This would be a programme on an 18-year timetable; or, if you are very lucky, 16 years. We don't realise that at all. For generation after generation, most of us failed to perfect it. All that parents really can do is to set them out straight in the world with some knowledge, but the idea is to go and beget them. I know that there are lots of pressures on parents, as we are told after realising the fact that they wake up and see the mess they got into and do the best of their ability to avoid not accepting that there are children around and you are supposed to educate them and all. Yes, it is very easy to feed them, clothe them, but for the education side it's very tricky. Parents don't want to get involved or even want to spend most of their time on their children. So, some think more or even come home very late not see them saying how busy they are on the TV, talk and it save them if they do come. Their only understanding is that everybody is afraid that their own kids will do what I was forced to do. It's not why or how it comes about; there are many people that will cross their family off the list for nothing.

Training for parenthood?

Such crimes are committed by parents because they have nothing to give. If there was an exam like a driving test to tell you whether you can have kids or not, it would be great. Some people are just useless as parents. You have to give so much attention.

The majority of all these problems are brought about by parents that were not made to become parents in the first place. Many people get married thinking they are freeing themselves from their parents, and run into a wall of brick without a hammer and chisel to cut through. Some of them have the power to go through without aid. Towards children it is hard; many are taught wrongly of the whole structure. With only a one-sided

CHAPTER 9: JACQUES' REFLECTIONS: PARENTING, CHILDHOOD, SOCIAL STRUCTURE

life, you have to do it my way – and then they see that their parents do it differently. It is difficult for the child to understand; but, of course, if the child is passive, then you don't have to worry. In my case, that wasn't the way I was. In many ways I was pushed into it via he Australian Jewish family structure. But those few years that I had on the Farm made a lot of difference to my path in life.

Jacques almost aways uses capital F for farm and I have retained this.

Those evil parents cannot cope with families or a minimum of pressure; it's a distasteful way to put it, this confronting thing in childhood. For the sharing idea of having themselves so in old age they will tend to their needs; well, they are very wrong indeed. The investment that parents put in is very hard. There are 18 years of worrying. Is it worth it? Not too many make it; somehow, due to precious commitment both sides, they don't fulfil their demands at all.

I can forgive a nation, but parents – never! I will never side with a parent if the child isn't properly loved, cared for, because of the selfishness of each of us. All we can do is produce in their eyes value repeated for them as we would for ourselves.

The evil is laziness and lack of forethought. In Jacques' view, it seems never to be malice or intrinsic evil.

Relations with friends and parenting
My friends hate me because I go straight to the problem. I don't try to make up any excuses why I can't or why it happened. The truth is what is important to me – nothing more. All I know is that I'm luckier than those kids that were with parents and had what they call a stable family life. As long as the parent thinks the child owes him something, then something is wrong somewhere. As far as I can see, a parent should be a parent; 99% are not that educated – they just follow what has been passed on to them like our forefathers. It's more like a business deal. Here I am,

talking about my mother, but this is in general. Believe me, I have been there. I got it first-hand. It's not from books.

Do you know that Diana is the only person that has admitted to me that she had a good childhood? All the other people I have met had horrible childhoods, with something that was missing, etc. Yet today they have kids, and their kids hate their parents. Yet they're caught in a box because they cannot ignore them because they got something from them, so they have to cope with their problems. Now, coming to what they have experienced, you would think they would not get married, but they think 'I can do a better job than my parents', which is a myth again. We are programmed to do exactly that: get married and ruin our short life thinking one is doing one's duty.

> *Jacques describing his experiences led to others remembering childhood desires not fulfilled and so m ay have led to his view that their childhoods were unhappy.*

Well, I have experienced marriage, and being childless is still good. The problem would happen when you have kids – probably.

> *He would have been such a great father, as he always listened, understood, and cared.*

Fear of having children
Today, like the past, the fear in me of having a family – children that I should bring up with understanding, love and care, to give all your time and patience to – isn't one of my best qualities. The fear that I'll be a failure as a parent hurts more deeply than anyone can imagine, since I don't have any knowledge whatsoever about family life to talk about.

> *I only wish I could have proved him wrong. I reiterate. He would have been a wonderful father, but I could not give him that. So, he was a*

CHAPTER 9: JACQUES' REFLECTIONS: PARENTING, CHILDHOOD, SOCIAL STRUCTURE

> *wonderful 'uncle' to every child he knew: friends' children, my niece and nephews. I cry every time I read this.*

I grow plants or fix a car; it's much easier than raising children. You can always sell the car and laugh off your mistakes. But with a very small child, you're faced with a constant challenge. I could say I'm too lazy to try; that would be the easy way, but man and woman are very lazy people. If more people thought like me, there wouldn't be children for those who cannot cope with problems. I don't mind failing in anything; except, with the handling of small innocent children, I really fear it. Even with my background, I have my doubts.

Education

Most children don't get the right kind of education. They start from an early age of getting the facts of life wrong, stories about what is true and what is a lie, which, of course, they don't understand very well. Teachers make it easier for themselves. But we still have to find a method that makes it in the education world; even for some children who are not made for the standard system. I may say no one has found a better system to satisfy the real need for such kids.

> *Teachers say, 'could do better'. A sorry admission of failure that has me reaching for a gun!*

We are different to others in so many areas. Everything is passed on to us by people that have received that same knowledge. The opportunity is there that we may take and continue the line. Yet many of us think twice about the knowledge passed on. If it is our livelihood, we keep secret what we need. There is no mystery about it that information or items are limited. As for me, I had to learn the hard way. 'We will tell you when you are older' was the answer from my widely educated family. But I went further.

Jacques saw that our current system is deeply flawed, but saw that a good solution is hard to find.

Learning as a child

My mind goes blank at times – nothing goes out or in. It took me a long time to understand that one has to learn everything not by theory but practice. I always thought that one has the ability of creating something for the world, but it isn't easy. Education doesn't tell you at an early age that you cannot really do anything in any subject unless you learn a certain subject following what is known. I have no doubt that teachers are too vain to sit down with pupils that look like they need the road to learning – like reading. I thought if there were as many people as possible that knew how to read, then it wasn't worth it for me to know how to read (others could do it). I wanted something special, which I never found. Man can only follow in the footsteps of his ancestors: merely modernising the technology. So, the next streak of science might be getting your car to drive, so you would be able to sit in the back playing whatever?

- Good old Australian music.

Little did he know how close we are now to that technology!

Shortcomings of education: Hebrew and secular schooling

Even today, the education is still bad. It doesn't tell you or explain in many ways why – not that it wasn't interesting enough. The past society brought this about, no less than the Second World War, which didn't achieve much for humanity really. It didn't stop the suffering that still ran on the road of life. Politicians are not better today than they have been in the past. They still can't solve the economic problem, which, of course, is the main problem.

Education should be there for those that find it hard to learn in a group. They need to get an individual tutor, since they are a very low percentage indeed. I'm sure that there are some so-called teachers which would better teach one child individually than in a class. Yes, till the child has enough knowledge to join other children in class; like this, you would have a rich population more able to work together.

This confusion that these children are put in is what I call a master crime that ruins them for life. It's not that there isn't any money about, but it's more laziness of the ruling class on the education, since we humans don't have the responsibilities that are there in the animal kingdom. We are left with but little hope for the future for us all. If man and woman hope to achieve some success, they must spend more time with those younger people that have been pushed out of our society. In many of us, the thought that we might have been healthier in mind is ever present. We look on anything that doesn't appear in our lives as dangerous as a novelty.

We train our children at an early age to hate, to be frightened, and this complicates everything that is built for us. At this very moment I can't do anything to help any small child, to educate them. One is confronted with a body that is moving very hard solely to adjust itself to the modern way; to be more specific, the fight of conservation – but even that is wrong. All our Western civilisation is dying for the sake of what? We have now an involvement in that death that is quite shocking. Some life, I must say, yet I'm lucky   it hasn't touched me yet.

> *These thoughts are not very clear, so I wish I could ask him. The gist is that education does not equip us for the very serious problems of our current world, including war and waste of talent.*

Here I am trying to justify all that has happened. I can only see that we wise, beautiful human beings haven't much changed for the good, but have put most of the blame back on the man on the street, with problems which really belong to the government of the world. They do hold the reins – don't they? – but do little to bring forth better education on the problem of children that are brought into the world, producing more misunderstanding than good.

I admit that many more people before me have tried to put across this unsolved problem by writing, or yelling out, 'Stop! Think for five minutes and look at how you are living.' The education world cannot and won't teach the young children the truth of life, except for useless things like religion and how to use less of your mind, and so making sure that you fit in the system. Further than that, if the child refuses to follow these steps, then he or she is outcast for the rest of their days in the family.

With me, my education came from meeting people and doing it, not reading those books that very few people can use for minor things. Yes, nobody understands Shakespeare; if they did, the family structure would be in a better shape than it is now. It's just good for one thing, relaxation and no more (what a laugh).

Foster families

Moving children from pillar to post
We all know that separation of small children between the ages of 2½ years to seven is very important. If they should be separated from their original parents, they should stay put till they are old enough to understand, not to be put under stress with mixed emotions like the change of the weather. It can destroy the day overnight. And, moreover, it didn't matter whether it was the right thing to do (to return me to my birth mother), so that it was as it was before the war.

I never had a childhood, as it was cut short at the age of seven years old. I was to experience in that period the religion, being abused mentally, abused sexually, abused to the end; you call criminals whatever. But it happens that their responsibility for the comfort I needed was very limited, just to their pleasure and timing. I never had anybody to look up to: teacher or relative, no one. Even now, things have not changed much. I still consider the family structure a flop. The trumpet-blower with their dramatic historic Victorian manner passes on not much information to one how things should be: like 'Do it my way or else'. We have made no progress in the field of laziness.

There will be many more wars, and still people do not come out without suffering from the aftermath. No group of people ever write this about children of war. Like cattle, they try and fit them back like nothing has happened.

> Jacques, as always, considers the child's perspective and welfare. The UK Refugee Council has guidelines on treatment of unaccompanied minors, but necessary resources may be lacking and so prevent the child's interests being paramount. Is the situation better or worse than after the Second World War? Are migrants from favoured countries prioritised (e.g. Ukraine v Afghanistan)?

My belief is that in the future we shall be flying about space, reaching for new Earth to pollute. All of us have a streak of runaway, or the feeling that over the wall is more beautiful or great; achievement is really how to fulfil your days, with less interference.

> 'You may leave here for four days in space, but when you return it's the same old place.' (Barry McQuire, 'Eve of Destruction'.)

What young children know and want
> Many people believe young children cannot evaluate complex choices, such as who they wish to live with. Psychological evidence is continually lowering the age at which abilities develop. My view, based on Jacques' writing (albeit retrospective), is that even five-year-olds understand a lot and should be consulted. Adults need to be highly skilled to elicit child wishes.

Maverick: A memoir of Jacques Kornbrot, 1938 - 2014

This theory of talking to children is just a myth. I wish I could have had some place where they would listen and help, but it was not so. I was crucified and branded a liar, which I'm not, or a thief, which I'm not. Yes, I was made to feel a useless person, and to me that is unforgivable.

Jacques' desperate need for someone to talk to is truly harrowing.

Many false things happened before my eyes. At an early age, I could tell between the truth and lies, something that is still with me till this day. Not being in the system in a group that helps one another – how nice it must be where you don't lose your privacy.

But foster parents can create great lives. Jacques' foster sister Denise married and created a great family in her turn.

Foster sister Denise, with: Jacques; Henri & 1st grandchild; children Christian, Martine, Francine; grandchild

CHAPTER 9: JACQUES' REFLECTIONS: PARENTING, CHILDHOOD, SOCIAL STRUCTURE

Intervention from outside
Back to Mars, a battle between the two, and I don't belong to either side, to no system at all. Yes, a lot of people tried to help, but it was only in their own manner. I was forced to be with this woman on the 6th floor, closed in a flat – my freedom was taken away. I'm quite surprised that I didn't get claustrophobia. As far as my logic and what I understand, they did their best to make me feel that I was a criminal. A parent will not understand that like a plant, if you don't water it or put it in the right kind of soil, then it won't grow right. Simple but true. If only I could say something good about them. They say Shakespeare was a genius, but he was just like any guy.

Changing family structure
I had to put up with the largeness of the family structure, and its action was to sweep everything under the carpet. I have coped till now, but this burden I have carried a long time is coming out. I can't stop thinking about it. I know that I have succeeded in convincing myself it was the right thing to do due to the incompetence of the family structure. Whether the cause is for those forced to marry due to financial gain or war or whatever, it's a strain. It's silly not to admit it's just one more wrongdoing than right; even after all these years, no one wants to understand my position, right or wrong. It does not matter what I say, nothing will change things – to many, all the family structure means is family. In my mind, the family is a failure. I can understand nations being cruel to one another, but not the family, which is a real lot of rubbish.

Jacques' adult reflections

Human nature
This is not part of the story, but something that people are or have a fear of: the loss of their secure life. What the neighbours say is very important. Yet it ignores that we create our own problems more than we can cope with. Many of us, 98%, follow their parent, making sure we can fill the

day with things we enjoy, and don't see further than this. Eighteen years or less or more with getting yelled at. Then you go away to start your own life to do the same that your own parents did themselves. One's education is fruitless, when you think that these people are supposed to make a better world for us, and us for them. Yet we are just as bad as our parents or ancestors. They know how it is useless; it is a waste of time for everyone concerned. You expect that someone that has spent many years learning would know better, but he is just as stupid as a person with no learning. The thing I could never accept is that you have to follow in the footsteps of your parents, yet we follow them. It is in our genes. All around us we have this illness of wanting to run away. We hope to come back with knowledge that would make everyone around envy you.

Influencers Willy, Kuba and Rahel, Bobby

There are no clever people. I know only phoneys that think they can do the job better, but it comes down to what we are. What it comes to is that if it's not economically sound, no one loves you or cares enough. We are not clever but very lazy, so lazy that we have created this wild dream that one day everything will be great. There will be no more war or sicknesses, all love and play. That's a lot of false dreams. The whole structure of any civilisation is to have control above it all. People, even when they crossed the 28 seas, did not go to create something new or bring anything those people wanted. There they found the same problems facing them. No doubt it would take a greater evolution transforming into creating a much more advanced way of thinking that put their thoughts into action. It does no good really as it says what must be done, but no one follows on, as so many books provide so many new ways. Still, we behave the same. The individual doesn't really exist in any level; we make ourselves believe what even our crafty politicians tell us. It doesn't work that an invisible item, a power, and structure of hope that cannot be destroyed by man's ability has never been heard or even experienced, for there are many contradictions with our past.

The problem is not, 'Where did we go wrong?' We are all criminal in a sense. Even giving out charity to those that have worked all their life paying the extra to see that after all the invisible one country gives you or makes you feel you are having on these about it should be good.

This is confusing. Reference to 'invisible' may be the thought that new ideas have been dramatically unsuccessful in challenging religious belief and superstition.

Society and religion

The foundation of all is our negotiation with the laws of society. The Bible is a good example of putting one into such a framework. We have dismissed it for a better way. Unfortunately, we have not achieved this better way. We are lost. We are still being led by the hand by those people behind the surface. There are leaders that we never see ruling the world planning – creating situations, making sure nothing became perfect like the Garden of Eden. As all religions claim, only God is perfect.

Those that follow their own code of rule not being bound by the public code will always be stung. Once you widen your actions or for some reason become confident, then you are as good as lost in the martial art of it all.

Building a better society

Kibbutzim
The whole structure of the kibbutz is quite complicated. Like any nation, the freedom of doing something of your own is limited. The whole kibbutz

is involved in decision-making to a certain point. Then it is the 5% ruling group that makes the final decision. None of them made any impression on me; with all their talking, they were not inventing something new. What I saw was them securing their future. Having, then, a ruling class, you can't have it differently than this: as much as you love equality of man, it is but a useless dream which never existed. As long as everyone follows the way I think, then you are all right. Good guys don't get to the top, ever.

Every Saturday night, where in the city people go out to enjoy themselves, on the kibbutz we had meetings over the past week. Information on what was gained for the kibbutz money-wise, and who wanted to go on a course, and maybe a new member is accepted.

When you get too many educated human beings in a group, it's for sure you will have problems. The *what* and *who* ways have to be worked out. Not too many of us have the power of speech to put over our case so everybody can understand this situation of how to run the show. In a group, everything becomes political – such is the way of life. Giving new hope of the golden rainbow in the end which isn't, as it won't help any.

> *Nevertheless, he was always optimistic, with happy action and laughter and a joy to be with. Serious and humorous discussions with friends from the army, kibbutz Negba Tel Aviv and Ashdod inspired reflections.*

Israeli friends, Mordi, Freda, Jacques and Ilana Wedding guests, Amitai, Danny

CHAPTER 9: JACQUES' REFLECTIONS: PARENTING, CHILDHOOD, SOCIAL STRUCTURE

Israeli friends, Avishai, Ilana, Dario, Gershon Abu, Druri, Ariella

What a life! You sit down and read all the best ways how to win, but in the end, there will be no solution. However attractive it may seem, we all play in that wheel somehow.

Building a nation: goals of immigrants

The amusement and sorrow of building up a new nation or country like the US and many new developing areas of Africa. Israel is a creation that gives hope to individuals to start a new life in a distant land, believing that it will be better than the old country. Like a new car, it feels good. And as they come to the Promised Land after many years away from its beauty, to build a new nation, their aim is to make a homeland where there would be no more antisemitism seen. No nation has ever been built without conflict with its neighbour. Wars were waged, many came and many left. I'm writing in particular about those that came from the free world of the West. For them, crossing borders was easy. Yet many fled their country, like the US or France, for the fear of being sent too far away. Wars like Korea, Indochina, Algeria. I do not have the correct figures, but many came and left in the same manner. They were dissatisfied with the conditions they lived in.

Maverick: A memoir of Jacques Kornbrot, 1938 - 2014

Technology to improve human life?
Well, technology only exists in the military way by producing better weapons of destruction; but in the field of day-to-day life, that has not got any importance whatever. I mean, the human race is deciding to take off to a distant planet, for this one is not lovely anymore.

Achievements

We grow up through stages – infant, then into boy, then into teenagers – where our frustration came for a long period of years. You become a killer for what? Whether your mind is at war or at another place, it doesn't matter either way. You want to become active, to show yourself. I sit or walk about with my thoughts, thinking that I'm luckier than those kids that were born with tons of silver spoons in their mouths, their future secure. The help and the comfort they got they rejected because it is not made out of gold.

The only person I really envy is my foster sister, Denise. How lucky she was to have been given to my foster parents. When we met again after 30 years, she longed to find out who her real parents were. I told her anybody that could have left her in the street like that was not worth knowing. I'm lucky that I have never had to take anything that was not mine.

Village versus city
Maybe it was the slow rhythm of those few years I had when I was on the Farm. Country people are more human than city people. They don't have to show what they are really not. In Paris, it was pushing here, pushing there; hardly any stopping in the street to speak to anybody. On the Farm, you would take your time; there was time to be taken. Out on the Farm, you wouldn't notice the night come early like you do in the city. Everything is time; you feel dark coming much quicker, probably because of the buildings and the lack of open space. I was full of wild thoughts,

CHAPTER 9: JACQUES' REFLECTIONS: PARENTING, CHILDHOOD, SOCIAL STRUCTURE

liking or wanting to do things that I couldn't do. Everything that was done for me, I revolted. I didn't appreciate anything, which was very strange.

Yet in the end he chose the city, although he was always happy visiting the country.

Looking back on Villeherviers
Yes, I have crossed loads of frontier religions, and all for the sake of living. This story that took place was one of a hundred thousand children like me that, after the Second World War, were reunited with the remains of their family. Of course, it was a disaster for me. I can't talk for the others, but that's the truth, and anyone that knows me from the time of 1945 till 1956 will recognise it was one big disaster.

Yes, from that little Farm and my little world of theatres, I was heading towards the greatest misery that I have ever received. What crime was committed against me is beyond any of today's dreams – and over time it still continues. As I say what is right and wrong as it was in my life, that is honest.

Jacques intuitively had a sense of right and wrong. It seems to me that most people do have that sense, but where does it come from?

Yearnings, up to finding Denise, Jacques' foster sister
If I could even see a photograph of that place for just a moment. It is so sad that I was taken away from that quiet lovely farmhouse where peace was in me two hundred percent, hour by hour. Unjust. But at that age one's point of view wasn't asked for; you just had to accept. I would've remembered things much more clearly today. Alas, it's not, as I have tried very hard to find that little place out there, one side of me wanting very much to find it and the other side just to remember it as it was put there in my mind. If only I could find that place now. I know my parents would have passed away, but my red-haired brother and my two sisters must still be living somewhere, somewhere in France.

Jacques finally found Villeherviers by visiting his old primary school in Paris, where they had records of his previous school! The reunion was dramatic and fantastic.

It was so nice finding my sister was not far away from where we all lived during the war.

Looking back on life

Well, there you go again, trying your best to understand the situation. Once again, we shall try to put down what it was that changed my whole way of thinking! Judging by the people that were supposedly the brains but had none at all. They were trained and knew when to bow their head when necessary! Heavens, the times I would have loved to kick their ass in for their small minds. Yes, my name is Jacques Kornbrot, one of the last few with a name like that. I have gone far from that little village in the Loire. When looking back at what one has done in one's life, it gets you to wonder what would have been the right things to have done or said.

Passing on experience

But, like those that have tried to pass on their experience, all of the ones talking about the way life should be have failed to pass on anything constructive. In practical things they have more success, due to the need of ours to put a brick on top of another. But as how one human can be made to love their neighbour, as well as how to teach the truth to the kid – they have done very badly. They start by lying to them about the most important thing in their education; the stories they are told will deceive themselves at the end of the day. By the time that you realise the truth, it's too late to change anything! But to be annoyed or bitter, as many people I know. Alas, I'm past that phase. I stopped a long time ago searching for justice. In a cunning way, it is everyone for himself, with the help of your surroundings: use and be used. Some are better than others. But when it really comes down to it, you do it, liking it or not. The

CHAPTER 9: JACQUES' REFLECTIONS: PARENTING, CHILDHOOD, SOCIAL STRUCTURE

truth is that dream, that awful dream, wanting someone fighting so that at the end you will be bowed to.

Hard for me to understand, but he never stopped dreaming and searching for justice. I could not help him. I weep that there were opportunities, perhaps many, I missed.

Life lessons
No one can tell me about life now, or the agony that goes through everybody's mind. The question is, 'Will I make it or not, will I be able to leave something to be remembered by?' It is the closing of my youth at the age of seven, standing at the door of the farmhouse, that I remember so well. I felt lost, like just before going to battle and not knowing if I shall ever return to my foster family.

Where I am now
Right, I guess I shall try again to explain myself much more clearly than before, since everybody thinks I am playing a game. Who is going to win and who is going to lose? I'm not playing anybody's game. If more than 30 years ago nobody wanted to understand what it was all about, then I am very sorry that people think that I'm just going to say, 'What a lovely person', etc. My law is as follows: there is not any love for anybody... or I care, or I don't care. I want to be left alone. I never got any joy from her; she only knows one thing, only to beg and cry her heart out; how she suffers, as though she's the only one in the world. There is so much that I cannot take of her deception and the way she convinced everyone what a son-of-a-bitch I was. Even now, she is crying on someone's shoulder.

It's like a bad dream that was actually happening to me. Now, with most of the information I have gathered together, I'm supposed to piece them in place so I should finally know as plain as that how I will cope with myself in future understanding of the dark shadow of my past. Yes, the past decisions I made, realising too late that it was the wrong one, hardly blinking an eyelid to correct it.

So here I am, sitting down, writing forward on and on, trying to put down what really led to my not wanting to continue correspondence or communication with the family. I don't understand any more about the right or wrong, but just to win in the short time that I have moved from society, meeting many lonely faces searching for an easy way to live their life out and leave behind a mark that they have existed.

Success?
I'm starting to wonder myself what it is to be a success. What is right, and how should you go about it? Real hell, this writing. The demands in our social structure, whether you like it or not, you have to be a bloody good liar, and cheat murder to end your days as a success so everybody loves you. What I am really getting at is that people are wrongly educated for their role of parent or managing other people's lives.

Now, after 30 years, the relatives that were useless then are still trying to convince me that I should write to her. But it is not enough. A parent should be a parent. Whatever, this myth of the child who is supposed to respect and obey is only if there is something to respect and obey about their lucky parent; but if your demands are stupid, like wanting things that you know or don't want to be able to pay back, well, there is not a thing you can do about it.

> *Jacques would have been 65. His cousin Ray, on a visit to us, tried to convince him to write to his mother. He absolutely refused. He did not want me to have any contact either. He felt she contaminated everything.*

Discussions with Wolfgang Reinhardt, father of Tom, son of Max
I recall when I was in Greece with Thomas Reinhardt. We met his father, and we talked about failure and success. I said I would love to have succeeded in something that I look back on and said I did well. He replied, 'I'm 54 and I still have not succeeded in anything.' I said, 'But you have many motion pictures behind you.' He still claimed he had not made it.

CHAPTER 9: JACQUES' REFLECTIONS: PARENTING, CHILDHOOD, SOCIAL STRUCTURE

Dreams
This isn't a misunderstanding towards the whole community, but the meeting of a group of people with their missed dreams who came about to make people believe that the future holds green colourful days where no one will ever suffer again. This is just rubbish. You can be money-wise, live a bit better off. But then sit down and listen to the word in the street that all have it better in some other nation or tribes or in any culture where, from king down, they had it good. This realisation has put us where we are now. You can't change this; it's just the way, dodging the major problem of our existence to give out.

Legacy of those who went before
I have never lived in a dream world. I fight it. It would be nice, but it destroys one's mind. It is hell for me to think that I reach so far, but I still have not accepted the rules of the society. I probably will never accept the fact that one must tell lies to keep everybody happy. That is not my style and never will be. To play the game; but what game? The religion game, the family, or the friend game?

So far, everything our ancestors have done is to produce more lies to educate the new brain about the world. As a child, I was made to feel that I was supposed to invent more than learning. That was my mistake of understanding, plus the fault of my teachers that did it wrong, like today. The more things are complicated, the easier they are; the method that our parents put across is wrong.

What if?
Things might have been different – alas, life is a long road, with many things along the way. Something that many regulars don't know is how to explain; or, in education, they only say I am right and that's it. I had more bad teachers than good ones, all those that were involved in their own problems. I was made the guilty party, partly because of my independent thinking. I won't change that much, either my taste for the open space and, of course, to be able to run.

Maverick: A memoir of Jacques Kornbrot, 1938 - 2014

Not to forget we were involved with the Second World War. What if the story about the aftermath had been different? Later, I look back at it and wonder if I would have been different if my father had lived and my mother hadn't recovered from her illness mentally.

What outcome would it have to sit back here and say 'if'? I must admit again that I have done quite a lot of adventurous things in my life, which only amount to a very small thing. I was a one-time idealist, thinking of no more than having a secure life for the rest of my days. But things don't really turn out the way it's written on paper. I was only 29 when I realised this. That, with all the modern technology, man still hasn't learnt anything since; we drop to earth even today and we are still forced to go making deals that bring us an advantage for more than we need. There will, of course, never be any change. We always think that it will be better tomorrow, the next day, month, year, but what we are doing is really making sure our neighbour doesn't gain more than us, as you sit back in a crowded corner saying, 'Well, let's be reasonable and do something new.' What now, new hallelujah? This isn't misunderstanding. People are waiting for that superman to give them an easy, comfortable life like someone else.

Even today we are still forced to go making deals that bring us an advantage for more than we need. There will, of course, never be any change. We always think that it will be better tomorrow, the next day, month, year, but what we are really doing is making sure our neighbour doesn't gain more than us, as you sit back in a crowded corner saying, 'Well, let's be reasonable and do something new. Hallelujah.'

> *Everyone does some wondering 'what if?'. I do less than most, as I have been lucky. I had a good supportive start in life and then, wonder of wonders, I found Jacques.*

All my dreams were shattered to pieces, and no one at the time could have helped because I wasn't important enough, like a bad investment.

CHAPTER 9: JACQUES' REFLECTIONS: PARENTING, CHILDHOOD, SOCIAL STRUCTURE

No one could see any good in me; even today they still see it that way, not wanting to know what is stored in that little brain and mind. Undoubtedly, they still wonder why, and still they do not come out with the right answer: admitting that they could have done better in bringing me up. Productivity was nil on both sides.

- I, Jacques Kornbrot, can only see what I can do today and not what will happen a hundred years from now.

Bitter reflections
When I die, I will be a bitter man. Whatever happens, in my mind I have given away everything for nothing. What gets me is I'm not the only one. Whether the excuse is family broken or war, no one really cares; everybody just tries to push the problem away.

> *So hard to admit, but Jacques was bitter in his last years. Although he talked about his bitterness, he did not actually act bitter. He always had fun with people. I note again: we laughed every day, and he did not pass his bitterness on to me.*

But it's hard for me not to cross people off the list these days. It's hard to look on the bright side of it.

> *Jacques was never violent, but if people failed to treat me or him in a way that lived up to his standards, they were 'off the list' – forever.*

Susie's kids have not done much with all their silver spoons in the mouth; one can't really say they have achieved much. How funny that those who judge me are being judged. But I'm not hurting greater damage. They say I'm hard. They surely don't give you a medal for failure, but my list of their incompetence is endless. Anybody. Just words, but, with all their piety, they really made no difference.

Maverick: A memoir of Jacques Kornbrot, 1938 - 2014

> *Irvin Rockman, son of Norman and Susie, who paid for Jacques to go to boarding school, became Lord Mayor of Melbourne and had three wives and was accused of drug trafficking.*

Wanting people to learn from his experiences
The more I write, the more comes out, flashing back as many things about all those lost years, yes how does one in any situation, so one can write down and make others understand through word that will just over into their heads all stored and forgotten. Human beings with their talent of listening, and I belong to them, too.

It must be months now that I have sat, laid around, figuring how I am to finish this book. It is very hard indeed to put everything down on paper the most honest way for others to understand what I have gone through all these years, dodging society, being one of the crowd!

> *Jacques started rewriting on 2nd June 1977, age 39.*

Since everything is one big contradiction, there are still many unanswered questions of why? How could this have happened to me in the first place?

In the last week, or as I have sat down and have lost the connection of my brain, I can't write any more through the fear of not being able to make myself understood on paper. It's a fear of knowing whatever I write, no one will take heed of my thoughts, reading the stories and, for what it's worth, the magazine, that the truth is more about what is happening outside of America. Probably to show the world that it is not as bad as other countries. A section of Australia, with its wave of new immigrants to the Promised Land, still has its horrifyingly sad episode. Such a rich country, yet the immigrants still live in the ghetto, where they have to struggle for their existence, and children are still put into classrooms without a knowledge of the language, which is going too far. The time that those children learn something, they have already lost years of studies; but what they have is a very strong pattern for sitting down. In Brazil, you have seven million kids without parents. That has nothing to do with the war, so where is the excuse, you may ask. Out of laziness, they solve it by killing them off. To me, it all starts from the family and greed. We humans cannot go further than our family that would be giving away papa bear, mama bear and the little bear. More than that, we invent our global problem. I remember very well, Suzie Rockman, the charity giver, or, more likely, the ten-second charity giver.

Jacques saw the evils of modern society in all parts of the world.

A loner and an outcast?

In two words, I want to be left alone. As the Jewish saying goes, I got no joy from you, and you all don't have joy from me. What can be said? I don't want to play this stupid game; no one gains any victory from this. Like I said, the family structure is a flop, my friends.

I want to be left alone. I never belonged to any form of structure. I'm a one-man show, and there is nothing you or I can do about it. Everybody can play whatever game they want, and think or say what they want. It won't bother me one bit, because morally I don't owe anybody anything, as nobody did anything but take the side of that lady. It's so interesting how parents stick together and do their lying *for* society, *for the* family; that is worse than the Mafia. There you know where you stand.

The desire to be alone is specifically to have no contact with his mother.

Being an outcast

You still become an outcast if you don't follow the laws of society. I never belonged to the system. Really, I was always on the edge of the field, looking in from time to time. Yet here I am; I have survived that long.

On the Farm, he simply felt part of the family, and being an outsider did not enter his head. Then his world fell apart; he was totally alienated by the childhood world of his mother and relatives, and felt an outcast from that day to the day of his death.

Summary: Diana

Jacques' writings are the only evidence of the legacy he wanted to leave. The message he was desperate to communicate was that children should not suffer. He had various messages to achieve that goal: about the role of motherhood and the responsibilities of parents, society at large and the institutions societies create. People who made particularly valuable comments on the Ms., in order that Jacques knew them, are Pat Petrie, Faustin Charles, John Long, Richard Wiseman, Rachle Msetfi and Alison Klayman (Kornbrot) for some pictures.

Contributors, Pat, Faustin, John Richard, Rachel, Alison

CHAPTER 9: JACQUES' REFLECTIONS: PARENTING, CHILDHOOD, SOCIAL STRUCTURE

We were both atheists by the time we were 10. A supernatural God simply did not make any sense to either of us. We were at one in our belief that there is no life after death. There are no Gods, ghoulies, or long-lost grannies. Although belief in such supernatural phenomena may motivate morality, heroism, and pro-social actions, it often has dire consequences. The supernatural elements are neither necessary nor sufficient for the benefits. We never directly talked about such things. We both had a strong belief in a morality that values the well-being of all human beings, and, to a lesser extent, other living beings. We just got on with making decisions we believed to be for the best as they came along.

Beliefs and values

We both had moral values about what makes a good person. Consciously or subconsciously, our beliefs and values influence our decisions. We shared a sense of right and wrong as applied to actions and people. Jacques' definition of a true friend was someone who could be relied on to come to your rescue at 3am in the morning. He himself was a true friend in that sense: he would go out of his way to help and be sensitive when help was needed. No turning a blind eye for Jacques.

Being an outsider

As an adult, he remained an outsider, but always had more than one circle of friends: 'four societies', as he put it. He was valued by people from these many different circles, and I think he knew this. But he still felt not just an outsider, but also an outcast. Maybe it was partly because he enjoyed such diverse groups and had possible allegiance to so many countries that he felt an outsider. Jacques was, nevertheless, an inspiration to all he gave so much to his friends and their children – the next generation. If only he could have realised how much he meant to so many. I also have always felt myself an outsider in spite of my very conventional life and upbringing. I have a scepticism about received wisdom and a search after truth.

Outsiders, outcasts, and progress

Thinking for oneself is the good part of being an outsider. I also have always felt myself an outsider, but not an outcast. Jacques felt himself an outcast rejected by society. That was a high price to pay for all the good his outsider insights contributed to the world in which he found himself. In my view, outsiders are indispensable to bring out the best in people and avoid the swing to populist autocracy as a defence against insecurity. It is the outsiders, the mavericks, who have the potential to advance human joy and progress on planet earth. Viva les differences, **all** *the differences.*

The future

I tried and failed to be more optimistic. I am still trying, in Jacques' memory. Of course, it is impossible for me to deny the decline from the hopes of 1945 and of the 50s and 60s, when we were young adults. There are security guards round synagogues and Jewish schools in the UK today. The Israelis have hundreds of Palestinians in jail without trial and ghastly misogynist religious laws deny equal rights to women and 'bastards', as well as to non-Jews. My nephew Richard is a part of that. Evidently, Jacques and I and his honourable parents were unable to prevent his extremism, so in my view we all failed. Jacques did not know of the Australian policy to dump refugees on an isolated island, or the current UK vilification of immigrants. He did not know of the current, 2023, war between Hamas, with its planned atrocities, and Israel, with its panicked disregard for collateral damage to Gaza and Israeli citizens. Not what he fought for. Not the democratic Israel our forefathers dreamt about.

CHAPTER 10.
LONDON AND MARRIAGE, THE FUTURE

This chapter aims to show how Jacques came to lead an honourable life that brought joy and enlightenment to the many people he encountered and befriended along his way. He overcame early traumas to be an inspiring positive force. We were able to lead a typical middle-class life with no worries about food or shelter and resources for enjoyment of socialisation, entertainment, leisure, and travel. We would wish all humans could be so lucky.

We lived together from January 1973 until Jacques' death. We laughed together every day, even when Jacques was fighting his demons (not that he told me). He was a great raconteur and companion, and his stories inspired me to think in new ways. We were deeply but silently committed to one another.

> *Personae at start* gives additional information about people who had an impact on Jacques' life, roughly in the order he met them.

Beginnings: early history and events

Wedding: 20th January 1973
My mother, Edmonde, organised *everything*: bridesmaids; ceremony at Hampstead Synagogue; cocktails at Painter's Hall; visiting relatives. Jacques arrived on 21st December from Tel Aviv, and I from New York City on the 23rd. Guests were diverse: friends and family of my mother and grandmother; my friends from school, university, and London; Jacques'

only London friends, three women he knew from a favourite Tel Aviv bar. My brother Tim gave me away and my brother Michael was best man.

Bride & Groom Family, guests

Starting off and finding a home

We started living together in a rental flat that Jacques and my mother had found in multi-cultural Kilburn, where we spent our wedding night. Then Jacques took off for work in France.

While Jacques was working, I found and fell in love with Elmhurst Avenue, in a North London suburb. I worried Jacques might not like the Northern Line running by the back garden, but he loved Elmhurst too! Our mortgage was six times the starting salary of a university lecturer (now it is worth at least twelve times the equivalent!). Jacques enthusiastically stripped ghastly floral wallpaper, painted the walls white, built cupboards, mowed the lawn, and planted flowers. We bought a double bed. The rest of the furniture was inherited and tastefully arranged by Jacques; much is still there. Happy days.

Leaving our wedding reception Full of hope. Ruth & Myke's wedding Tim, Lynn, Myke, Ruth, Jacques, Diana Ruth's cousin Katy

Employment

Jacques' employment

Jacques had lots of experience: agriculture, fisheries, construction, and, of course, the Israeli army, but no formal qualifications. His initial employment was landscaping central areas of assorted French motorways. He exercised his French on a galaxy of ministers and bureaucrats. I joined him and his boss Laurie[61] of BWD, with partner, Wendy, in Paris for the first of many fun days together.

His next project was landscaping a disused lead mine in Rhandirmwyn, a rural Welsh village, a bit of a culture shock. He was offered drinks far into the night (enabling unlimited opening hours). He declared (in a postmistress-connected call) that 'the village is called Randy Worm [Rhandirmwyn, insisted the postmistress]. They believe in home rule for Wales and have crossed out all the English signs ["What's wrong with that?" the postmistress queried].' Love talk was limited by the postmistress acting as gooseberry. Then there were London renovation jobs where Jacques made good friends with the workforce, mostly Irish and appreciative of Jacques' humour. Sadly, BWD failed, but we remained good friends with Laurie[61] until he died in 1990. After that, Jacques did not find meaningful paid employment that made use of his many talents. So, he devoted his time, energy and talents to becoming an eclectic collector.

My employment

My main career was at Hatfield Polytechnic (University of Hertfordshire), specialising in cognitive psychology (mathematical models of decisions) and statistics. I progressed to Head of the Health & Human Sciences Research Institute and a Professorship. Along the way I supervised 18 PhDs, and many progressed to high-powered careers. I attended and ran conferences, with interesting collaborations across the world, and had opportunities to travel with Jacques. I was a happy jobbing scientist.

CHAPTER 10: JACQUES AND DIANA, LONDON, 1972-2014

Jacques the collector

Jacques became fascinated by, even addicted to, the car boot sales and charity shops he discovered on his meanderings. So, he embarked on a new life as an eclectic collector. Initially, he restricted himself to £3 per item, latterly increased to a princely £5. Our good friend John Long[810] has curated some of the results on his meaning for all blog. Jacques had found a metier as a visual and conceptual creator. He was determinedly universalist, Christian (popes), communist (Lenin, Marx), and Eastern icons. He was the antithesis of curators who cowardly close collections for fear of being unwoke. Jacques wanted his collection to cover *all* cultures, whether he approved or not.

Cabinet, masks, staircase with ugly mugs study, ornaments, wall Conservatory different walls.

Jacques' formal education had been a disaster, so he felt he might have missed out on his true vocation. He made collecting his own. The house has African wood masks, aboriginal paintings, Mexican artefacts, sculpted heads, ugly mugs and all sorts of ceramics, metal work, and jewellery.

Eccentrically, the garden has robust chairs, with mannequins wearing my discarded clothes, a model in a helmet on a moped, miners' lamps, shining reflecting CDs on the shed wall; a chess set, a road warning sign, lamps, and curios.

Garden evolution

Jacques had a keen eye for the photogenic, as well as for collecting exotic cameras. Wherever we travelled, our first task was to find a 24-hour developer. I have drawers full of photos yet to be albumized. Since the digital age, I have more than 1000 jpegs. Ears and eyes are not neglected, every genre, every country: about 2000 CDs, 300 vinyl and 100 or so VHS.

Jacques the explorer

Jacques loved to drive. We explored all over the UK: cities, seaside, countryside. He became a knowledgeable and entertaining tourist guide. Kenwood, Verulamium, and Hatfield House were local attractions for our many foreign visitors. He took Bobbie[59] our great entrepreneur friend from Tel Aviv, further afield: Stonehenge, Cornwall, Tintagel. He ended up having seen more of the UK than I, the native.

Finding Jacques' foster family[4] – Denise

Our first great travel event was finding Jacques' foster sister Denise[41]. We visited every Villevielle in France (that was how we interpreted Jacques saying Villeherviers). We camped all the way and, notably, met the Gadoulets (vintners, African Eurocrats) in a village near Lons le Saunier. Jacques eventually found Denise's address via his Paris primary school. Our first visit we stayed at Romarantin Lion d'Or. Denise and Jacques fell into each other's arms, and 30 years of separation melted to nothing. We met her husband and children. Jacques had regained his childhood family. Denise and Henri visited us in London and had 'posh' lunch at Grandma's. Henri insisted on using his trusty pocketknife, to Jacques' amusement. Denise, so energetic and powerful, sadly ended her life with Alzheimer's. At least Jacques did not see it. Francine[42] (Denise's daughter) took me to scatter some of Jacques' ashes on the land near the farm in Villeherviers, where he was so happy and made others so happy. Pictures of Denise's successful family are in chapter 9.

Maverick: A memoir of Jacques Kornbrot, 1938 - 2014

Europe and USA

Leisure and conference work trips took us to France, Switzerland, Italy, Portugal, Spain, and Scandinavia. On a trip to Copenhagen, Jacques found Henning Mortensen[511] (a writer and Kibbutz Negba volunteer) via a bookstore and publisher. Jacques described the striking book cover (hands clasping large detached breasts). We found Aarhus via the Esbjerg train from an outstretched map (bemused Danes watched). The Harwich-Esbjerg ferry provided excellent food and a casino.

Travel, Jerusalem, France, Negev Florence relaxing, Negba

We visited NYC for my PhD thesis defence, where Jacques met my Columbia[10] friend Jock[82] who offered us a flying trip, refused by Jacques, after Jock explained how he fudged a night vision test. He died in a crash, teaching night piloting. We did a mega Greyhound trip to Los Angeles via Bloomington, Bowling Green, and San Francisco. Serendipity found us a Joni Mitchell concert on the Pacific highway. We stayed with the Los

Angeles Finkelsteins[1.2] several times and learned of early 19th century immigration and early entrepreneurship from Reuben[14] (rich disposer of defunct cars). We drove to Las Vegas, where Jacques enjoyed the gambling, and to Tijuana, Mexico, via San Diego (gambling). There were no obvious migrant problems at the border then.

We experienced many places and people. It was exhilarating and challenging and exposed us to how little we knew or could know of even the places we visited. Travel broadens the mind and exposes its potholes. Jacques never felt himself tied to any one country, while I am quintessentially British. We both aspired to be citizens of the world.

Jacques, maverick inspiration

Children

Jacques was a pivotal adult in the lives of our friends' children. They saw an adult different from their parents with a perhaps exotic life. They sensed Jacques cared and they may have been able to tell him things they could not tell anyone else. My brothers' children all describe how much their lives were affected by Jacques. There are too many fun incidents, and perhaps profound discussions, to recount. The Petrie boys[7.1] next door saw Jacques as fascinating, as did our friends, Ian[6.3] and Theresa's children, who Jacques woke up to play with on weekends. We taught the kids of Dalia[8] (KAS school friend) to programme the video and played with them on the heath. Jacques was near godfather to KAS friend Juliet's[8] Polly, and missed her after her parents' toxic marriage crash led Juliet to cut us off for several years. Jacques did not forgive, because I had been hurt. The Mortensen Danish kids played croquet on the lawn. 'What does "sheet" mean in Danish?' we enquired. 'That is what Jacques says as he mishits the ball,' explained Henning.

Maverick: A memoir of Jacques Kornbrot, 1938 - 2014

Theresa, Ian, Rachel, Tim, Ian &Theresa, Muffi, Rachel, Diana & Rachel, Tim and Teresa.

Adult friends

Jacques was somewhat of a father figure to adult men. He was close to Ian,[6,2] who built our conservatory and then our bathroom. They had such fun together designing and chatting. On our 2013 trip to Limerick, Jacques especially connected with Muffi[89], Rachel's[88] Moroccan, French-speaking husband. He was another, originally French- (and Berber-) speaking practical person married to an English-speaking academic. Tim Maclagan who owned the ski shop that was the source of the garden skis was the most important local friend. After he retired they visited Muswell Hill every afternoon and regaled passers-by with humour from outdoor cafes

Neighbour Loulla gave exercise sessions and an insight into the orthodox church, while while David and Jane Sagal[56] provided Jewish links, and Pat and Glen Petrie Catholic perspective. Thus Jacques, the eclectic atheist, might have had Catholic, Greek Orthodox and Jewish gods watching over him. Richard and Helen Pettifor donated bird-nest boxes and sound advice. Sue Loughnane and Simon Kavanagh were other people whose company Jacques enjoyed. Ian Woods, who built the conservatory, and his wife Theresa and their children were an illuminating part of Jacques' life.

Time and his wife Teresa, Ian and his wife Theresa and Muffi and Rachel and my good neighbours continue to take care of me to this day – a tribute to Jacques.

Jacques' many societies

Jacques always had many societies. In Australia it was the family and Jewish community, Ballarat Grammar, local Melbourne gangs, and Joe's Café. In Israel it included his Tel Aviv aunt's neighbours (Ilona and Avishai), the local pub, workmates, the army, several kibbutzim, and Ben Gurion University intellectuals.

In Africa it comprised African and international colleagues, and polyglot expats with whom he frequented embassies. One anecdote even has an elephant dropping by his tent.

> What mattered to Jacques was people caring for others.
> Generosity not genes.

Family[1]
We slotted into a traditional family life: Saturday lunch with Myke[12] and Ruth[13], and their sons Ben and Alex, at grandma's and then at my mother's. Jacques immediately adopted Granny, fixing lights and things about the house, and Edmonde, fixing her car, and more. They both loved and were loved by Jacques. He listened and cared. Perhaps he wanted to prove

that bad relations with his own mother were not *his* fault. Love was so heartfelt and genuine; the reasons hardly matter. Grandma, active to the last, died of a stroke in 1978 while we were in Eilat. At the Shiva (Jewish 7-day celebration for dead relative), attended by diverse people, Jacques told Ernst Chain that the Mexicans invented penicillin!

Mother died in 1993 of a recurrence of breast cancer. She would have liked to have been a writer and did, indeed, write a detailed account of her family history. She had battled through the war on the home front and then worked with her father at his exclusive fur business. After losing both her father and husband in 1966, she worked as an administrator at British Titanium and then became Deputy Director of the British Friends of the Hebrew University of Jerusalem. She was committed to the Jewish community and had been President and Director of the London branch of the B'nai B'rith. I wonder what the older generation would have made of the world as it developed from such high hopes after the Second World War.

My brother Tim[11] was an engineer, management consultant, and art gallery director, and lived in Scotland with his family. His wife Lynn was a Glasgow GP, and they had two sons, Richard and Philip, and a daughter, Nicola. The family stayed with us at Christmas, and we returned visits to their home, first in Eaglesham and then in Newton Mearns. Tim died of colon cancer at 53 after a three-year battle (predicted 11 weeks – he really fought). The diagnosis came as mother lay dying, but bravely he managed a final visit before her death. My brother Myke was a very successful lawyer who had some influence on trust and tax legislation. Amongst other things, he was an author, article writer, editor of a professional journal and a founder member of the Academy of Social Sciences (having been nominated by the Society of Legal Scholars). His wife Ruth[13], a first-class lawyer, was ready after school each day to inspire their sons' childhood. She was a magistrate dealing with crime, matrimonial and juvenile issues, and is now an indispensable social and community pivot person. Jacques listened to her insights. Myke retired early and continues to use his skills for charities in Nepal, a local U3A and several others. Their sons are Ben and Alex.

More distantly, Grandma's French nephew, Raymond who had survived Auschwitz, had a special feeling for Jacques, whose father did not survive. Jacques adopted our elderly cousins Georgette (Raymond's sister) and Regina Pinto[17]. As was his wont, he listened, and they became friends. They were all important to Jacques.

Family occasions were always stimulating. There were games on the lawn; tourist expeditions; discussions, sometimes serious, sometimes fun, sometimes heated and penetrating, and the kids listened and had their tuppence worth. Acrimony was rare, and all views were entertained, Jacques' views being somewhat unique.

No children of our own

I was not able to give Jacques the opportunity to be a father. I was so desperate to have his children. So, I cried once a month for 20 years; not that Jacques ever saw, but he knew how much I cared. He was quietly empathetic, and patient throughout the abortive medical trials that found no defects in either of us. It was just not to be. Given the choice between having Jacques and having children, Jacques always came a long way first. I believe, and trust, he knew that. Infertility was tough for me, and we saw other marriages break up partly over fertility problems. We were committed to each other. I was often asked, 'Why not adopt?' A weird question! I only wanted Jacques' children. Not having them is the single major misery in my life.

Bristol[9] and professional[8] friends

My friend Carole[91] gave dinner parties, so Jacques met my Bristol friends. She had been a professional editor and had been enormously helpful on earlier drafts of this book. She succumbed to pancreatic cancer in 2022.

Valerie[92] has been a stimulating companion since my early post-university days, with an exciting Chelsea flat.

University of Hertfordshire Hatfield friends included, among others: Richard Wiseman[85]. with a quirky humour (my mentee and collaborator), who has provided invaluable insights on this book; Lia a Georgian who gave us great insights on our trip to Tbilisi, Mike Page[812] (climate activist, eco house builder), whose wife Birgit found Nobel Laureate Modiano had a family connection to Rue Bachelet, where Jacques lived from 1945 to 1948; George Georgiou a cyber psychologis. Rachel Msetfi[88] now Vice-president of Research at Maynooth University, has become an especially dear friend. We had a wonderful visit together to Limerick. Rocky the dog became Jacques' boon companion, and we visited the countryside with her husband Muffi[89] and daughter Zara, fed the ducks, and almost got drenched in the lake slithering on a dock..

Schoolfriends from King Alfred School (KAS)[7]
My KAS friends provided another diverse society for Jacques. Juliet[73], my school best friend, enjoyed TV and company with us before her marriage. Dalia[71] a KAS friend, married Faustin Charles, a Caribbean writer who has been extremely helpful with this book. Riva[74] (Joyce) was a passionate left-wing activist (died being expelled by Starmer's labour party 2021), and disagreements with Jacques were informative.

Kornbrot paternal family[3]?
Some 20 years ago, I got an email from another Dr Kornbrot in Philadelphia. 'Are we by any chance related?' she asked. It was Anna[31], the second daughter of Polish Holocaust survivors and the first female engineering graduate of Columbia College and later a maxillary surgeon. Anna's parents come from a small village. I have not been able to discover anything about Jacques' father, born in Warsaw, where many records were destroyed.

CHAPTER 10: JACQUES AND DIANA, LONDON, 1972-2014

Diana, Jacques, Alison, Barry, Diana, Anna, Jacques Mathew Ana, Barry, Alison Amy, Anna, Barry, Mathew

Their daughter, Alison[32], did a semester at LSE, and her parents, Anna and Barry, stayed with us at the start of their family European tour. They got on like a house on fire with Jacques, who emphatically did not care about family blood connections. For him, only friendship and character mattered. We became firm friends. Alison became a successful documentary producer (Ai Weiwei, women's basketball, Abercrombie & Fitch, etc). She was often in London and took great photos of us and the Elmhurst Avenue house.

> Generosity not genes.

Israel

1974 Yom Kippur War
Jacques was truly conflicted. We watched the TV sitting on the edge of the bed. He started on my right, telling me all the reasons he wanted to go back and join the fray. Then he bounced to my left while he reviewed (obvious) reasons for staying put. Unconvinced, he bounced back to the right, thinking of his mates. He spent several minutes as a human yo-yo. I do not know if he had residual guilt. The Israelis did fine without him, but then ruined chances of peaceful settlement for decades to come. Winning wars is the easy bit; subsequently winning the peace is tougher – Iraq, Syria, Eastern Europe, India, Kashmir, etc. etc. The current (2023) horrendous situation in Gaza is not what Jacques was fighting for. We would both like to see a secular democracy 'from the river to the sea'; not a Hamas-driven Sunni Islamic state, with no rights for Shia Islam, let alone Jews, Christians or atheists, women or LGBT; not a right-wing Israeli state with no independent judiciary, no rights for Arabs of any stripe, or indeed secular Jews, legal discrimination against women.

Visits and visitors
Jacques visited Israel almost every year, and I most years. We made the rounds of all his societies, and lived well on Jacques' disability pension (deafness, embedded bullet back pain). Negba friends visited London as guests or part of their plastics (now defunct) factory-related work. There were visits in both directions with Bobby[59,], originally from New York. There were vibrant discussions: New York and London activists had different views of Israel.

CHAPTER 10: JACQUES AND DIANA, LONDON, 1972-2014

Through the years Jacques. Jacques and Diana

Bobby also had no children. I pictured the three of us fading into the sunset together. It was not to be! She died of complications from diabetes after tough last years. Now there is just me. At least Jacques did not suffer much physical pain. Mental agonies, who *knows*? He protected me. If only I could have done more. *Crying again.* We also exchanged visits with Australian, Danish, and French friends. Gene Galanter[181] (PhD supervisor) spent a Sabbatical year with me. Jacques found him interesting, despite politics a bit to the right of Genghis Khan.

Willy[51] and Eilat

When Jacques was seconded to Kibbutz Eilot in 1957, he re-found Willy Halpert (now 90), the founder of the Eilat diving club Aqua Sport. Willy had known Jacques in Melbourne and recounts stories of Melbourne Jewish gangs. Apparently, Jacques was the favourite humourist of the toughest gang leader, although not a member of the gang (always a loner). Willy and Jacques became lifelong friends. We visited most Springs until Willy[51] moved to Toronto. Our Aqua Sport room enabled leaping straight out of bed and into the sea. Jacques loved walking around Aqua Sport's Coral Beach. Visitors regarded him as the warden or even owner. He was always very friendly but authoritative. Once a panicky lady was standing near the water, yelling for help. She said she had lost her diamond ring opposite where she stood. Jacques calmed and reassured her. She sat down very anxious, and Jacques said that no one was to enter there and disturb the bottom. He eventually found the ring further away and gave it to the lady. She ran away yelling thank you. All the onlookers thanked Jacques and said, 'What an awful person' – and worse. Jacques smiled and said, 'I hope she will be happy.' He did a lot of other things at Aqua sort, reminding people not to forget their towels and to pick up their litter by saying, 'The garbage can is over there – now you know where it is.' He always did it in such a friendly and smiling way that the teased ones became his friends. He really enjoyed ruling the Beach in his own way. Willy called him an Agent Provocateur. I just sunbathed with a good book.

Willy often visited London, and we had fun with his wife Maralyn, and her London cousins. We viewed Willy's film of him ending up in a Melbourne orphanage. Before Israel, Willy was a successful Melbourne engineer. He visits London often and we talk a lot about Jacques.

Army friends and kibbutzim

Jacques was especially close to Mordi[52] Zorea, who lived in Holon (Tel Aviv) on a super-social street. We enjoyed his family life. Such fun to show them all London, although Mordi found Elmhurst Avenue *much* too quiet. Jacques kept in touch with Israel by Skyping army friends every afternoon. We picked up with Jacques' previous girlfriend, Ilana (nearly wife). She had children, but no easy life and died in 2023.

Jacques was a worker, but not a member, on Kibbutz Negba. Kuba[54], a kibbutz founder, veteran of the English army in Egypt, and Mapam Knesset Member, was the nearest thing to a father Jacques ever had. They discussed everything long into the night. Later, I too learned from Kuba about kibbutz pioneers and their hopes (now in tatters). Sex stereotypes were rife. Women had to fight to drive air-conditioned tractors. Many mothers hated the decision (left male dogma?) for infants to sleep away from them in a nursery.

Entertainment

Jacques loved to entertain with humour, anecdotes, food, and drink. His cooking was original: pièces de résistance included chilli con carne and coarse-cut potato pancakes. Always delicious, but never the same twice. He loved to experiment, singing to himself as he invented. Our conservatory was always open house.

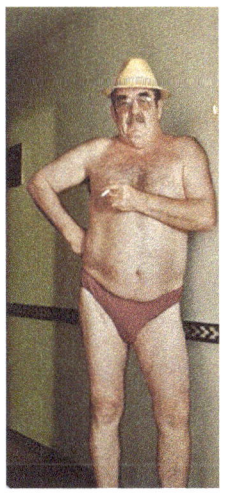

Jacques in many poses

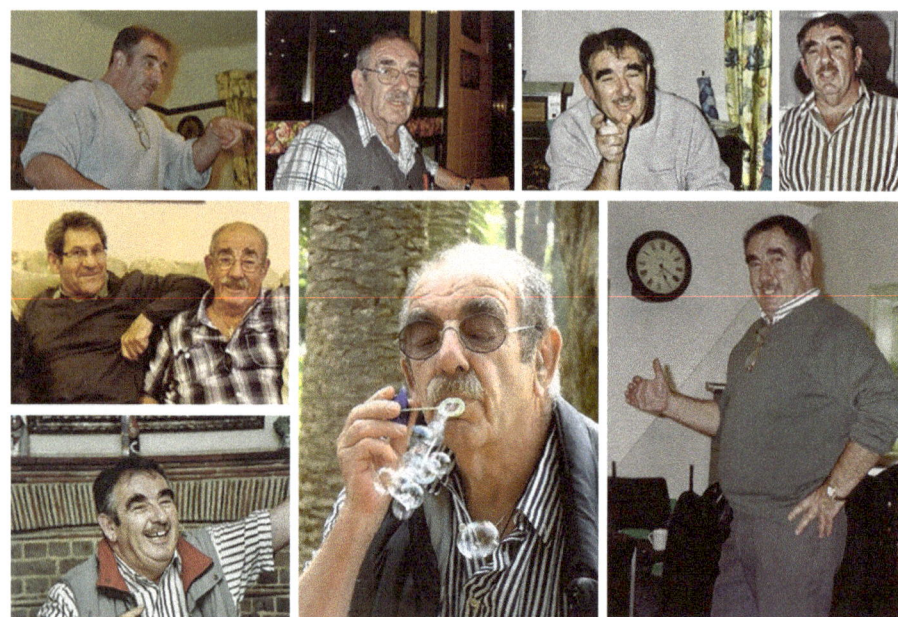

Jacques in many poses

Jacques was not one for joining anything! But he liked going to the gym in the early morning and swimming up to a mile a day. Initially, it was the Laboratory (I discovered in the 90s as a building site). After some lack of respect, we moved to David Lloyd with outdoor swimming, just a 2km walk away. Jacques, of course, made many friends, and I started rowing. Our gym friends supported me through Jacques' death and Covid-19 and helped me to a one-minute world veterans' record. We also did all the London culture stuff. We were members of the Tate and British Museum, theatre, films (notably *Tom Jones*, *Anna Karenina*, *Lawrence of Arabia*), music. Jacques enjoyed gambling as an occasional amusement: poker with the boys in Israel, the casino in our luxury Istanbul hotel, and slot machines on various ferry trips. It was always well under control.

CHAPTER 10: JACQUES AND DIANA, LONDON, 1972-2014

Ending and Beginning

Where we started

We both had loving families and opportunities for self-expression for our first seven years, even though the adults around us were beset by the Second World War. Then Jacques' world fell apart when his mother arrived and took him away from his loving, competent foster family. He effectively grew up alone with no adults to turn to. He survived, but missed out on formal education, and much else. I, meanwhile, had all the opportunities of a middle-class Western child. Yet we made a committed and unified pair.

Where we ended

All Jacques' house and garden artefacts are lovingly relocated to accommodate renovations. They remain to inspire and comfort me. Some

Jacques' tree 2024. Surrounding roses, winter.

of his ashes nourish his tree, perhaps communing with the Northern Line. The rest will one day mingle with mine on Hampstead Heath. Symbolic, but meaningless.

Jacques made an inspiring life after an idyllic start, followed by a disastrous later childhood. I was so lucky to have met him and to have been able to share his life. I hope others may be inspired and see hope for the future, despite the problems currently faced by all humanity.

Loss

We are no Macbeths, but Shakespeare tells of the anguish of the loss of an inspiring partner like no other.

> He should have died hereafter.
> There would have been a time for such a word.
> Tomorrow and tomorrow and tomorrow
> Creeps in this petty pace from day to day
> To the last syllable of recorded time.

Coda

Rest in peace, whatever that means. We live on, perhaps by this book's readers and surely in the hearts and minds of everyone who Jacques amused, stimulated, and inspired.

www.ingramcontent.com/pod-product-compliance
Lightning Source LLC
Chambersburg PA
CBHW042320090526
44585CB00024BA/2662